CHOSEN VESSELS

THE UNITING OF AMERICA'S PROMISES BEFORE THE SEMIQUINCENTENNIAL

CHOSEN VESSELS

THE UNITING OF AMERICA'S PROMISES BEFORE THE SEMIQUINCENTENNIAL

Elizabeth Grady Branch, EdD

PROJECT STAND-UP BOOK PUBLISHING

Fort Worth, Texas

CHOSEN VESSELS

**THE UNITING OF AMERICA'S PROMISES BEFORE
THE SEMIQUINCENTENNIAL**

Published by
Project Stand-up Book Publishing
Fort Worth, Texas
drebranch@aol.com

Elizabeth Branch, Publisher / Editorial Director
Yvonne Rose/Quality Press.info, Book Packager

Dedication

My Dedication bears a message of love and hope that we must continue to send throughout our nation. To my dear friend, Opal "Grand Mother of Juneteenth" Lee, I especially would like to include a dedicatory notation. Thanks so much for being my friend through so much of this project. May God continue to bless you and yours.

Chosen Vessels is also dedicated to our dear young African American scholars (and their friends of all races) who are in search of ways to make life in America a better country for a diverse population, now, in commemoration of the Semiquincentennial, and in the future.

Many of your ancestors were not faced with these same obstacles, but there were many other hindrances placed in their way. Even though they faced many battles against discrimination, hate and inequities, they pressed forward, too. They could have quit, but they didn't. They did not give up. They are the shoulders we all stand on today as you continue to overcome some of their adversities. Your ancestors would be proud of your talents and skills, and I am proud, too. That is why I am dedicating this book to you. That is why I, and others, continue to write and teach against hate and poverty. As proud Americans, we must continue to look for the opportunity to allow others "to stand on our shoulders."

I am dedicating this book to you. You are the reason people like me keep writing. I thank God there are many others like you out there, and I love you all. But you are the ones I know upfront. Yes, I love to "name drop" and take pride in having played a positive role in some small and meaningful way in your young lives. I remember when you were subjected to gangs, drugs, crime, street violence, and many other acts that could have caused you to lose focus, but you hung in there. You did not give up. You made wise choices. You are now internationally known "history makers" who have touched many lives that I know and love personally. You are living representations of the hopes and dreams of our ancestors as far back as slavery times! I want to say thank you! Thank you for continuing to motivate me and making our ancestors proud!

> To Kirk "Gospel Music Mogul" Franklin, one of my husband's 'favorite unforgettable' former Anatomy students at O, D, Wyatt High School,

> To David "Mister Brown"/Actor/ Producer Mann, my son Marcus's buddy growing up in our "Rolling Hills" 'hood,

> To Tamron "Talk Show Host Great" Hall, my daughter-in-law's (LaMildred Seay) 'Luling, Texas' cousin,

> To Cora "Author/Pastor/ Businesswoman" Jakes, one of my favorite teenage 'phone to ear' young office assistant and youth advisor at our Man in the Mirror non-profit office, and

> To Darla "ABC7-WABC NEWS TEAM, NY, (4 x EMMY awards recipient)" Miles, one of my daughter Bethanye's best "buds" at O.D. Wyatt High School in New York.

I also dedicate this book to my family and friends; and hope that you will continue to discuss and share this book with your friends for many years to come.

Contents

Acknowledgements

I want to thank our Supreme Being for His Divine guidance in writing this material. It was truly my desire to offer helpful, truthful, non-toxic materials that would teach against hate. I wanted to provide hope and a desire to continue to "rise and build" in spite of adversities and the reasoning behind them. At the same time, I knew I should say what needed to be said to our young scholars. So, I was prayerful, said it, and did it…I shared what I deemed important to say.

Sometimes, that can be difficult, but let me paraphrase a little, "We can do all things through Christ, who strengthens us." (Philippians 4: 13). I want to acknowledge everyone who listened to my dreams and served as witnesses, sometimes unknowingly, to what I thought and did during the composition of this project.

Special thanks to my sister, Lola Grady Campbell, a retired educator; my friends Linda McSwain, Dione Sims, Donald Williams, and Audrey Irving for your encouragement and help in making "Chosen Vessels" happen.

I must also acknowledge some other family members who have always been "the wind beneath my wings:" Forrest and Lillie Mae (Wesley) Grady and children (Doll, Faye, Rene, Dess and Phillip);

James Sr., James Jr., Marcus, Bethanye, and grandchildren (Kwonie, Meecie, Staci Rae-Rae, Bre, and Nova).

Thank you again and again, family and friends of the Branches. Most of all, I thank God!

To our dear young and dynamic American scholars,
I hope you are ready and willing to engage in
this serious faith-based dialogue …

INTRODUCTION

Making America A More Perfect Union

I, Elizabeth Grady Branch, octogenarian, and author of "Choosing to Lift Every Voice and Sing," agree that, intentionally and/or unintentionally, love and hate can be taught. As a faith-based author and semi-retired educator, I choose to teach love. I want to teach love, hope, and unity. My faith dictates it! I believe that our great country, America, needs it to survive! I know we cannot eliminate every bit of hate and divisiveness in the country, but we can all try. My work in this generation, just as our ancestors before us, will make a difference!

I hate to offer this dire and grim forewarning, but I must. Hate and divisiveness can destroy this democracy. It will destroy your hopes and dreams for your future. Our ancestors sacrificed too much for us to ignore or allow racism and divisiveness to control and manipulate your place in society. Prepare to fight, intelligently, with knowledge, truth, and self-determination! I want to help you and your friends (of all races), to defend yourselves with our chosen contributions of historical and lived experiences. Abraham Lincoln once stated, "Most nations don't die from invasions, they die from internal rottenness."

Our nation of diverse peoples cannot continue to thrive with racism and hate. It is an "internal rottenness" running rampant and unchecked. If you love and cherish America, as I do; and you want to pass on to the next generations an even more improved and blessed country, join me on the journey to unite these States filled with diverse Americans!

As we approach the Semiquincentennial, in 2026, the timing for my dialogue and action is perfect. Our diverse population is growing larger daily. We can review some of America's strides and struggles as a world leader. Together, we can determine how weak or how strong our nation has been over the past years, and, as a result, our future can be even brighter.

I want to share some of our true lived history and beliefs about our promising democracy; and I want to share the courageous work of a few of our Black and White American founders and ancestors' commitment and sacrifices to our nation.

Of course, there were many hundreds of thousands more who tried, heroically, to help make America into "a more perfect union." I wish I could share many more of the names, societies, clubs, and organizations who have struggled to help. Unfortunately, we don't usually highlight the fact that Blacks and Whites in America have always worked together to rid America of racism and divisiveness. Early churches in America, the Quakers, Unitarians, Methodist Ministers, and other clergy spoke out, adamantly, against the horrors of slavery. Many times, they did not win their battles, but they never gave up. Please know that many people of all races tried to make a difference by working in unity. Together, without divisiveness and hate, efforts were put forth to fulfill *the idea* of the United States of America. It is so important to me that I share with you that *the location* of America (not necessarily under that name) has been here since its Creation. But *the idea* of America, brought forth by our founding fathers, is what we celebrate as citizens of this great diverse country! It was established, in print, for all of us, in the Declaration of Independence, the US Constitution, the Amendments, and other documents that followed. This supposedly changed for us, our 1619 status as an enslaved Black race to an emancipated citizenship. Unfortunately, America has not fulfilled her promises, but has continued to pursue, Black and White, together, in unity, the enactment of equality and freedom for her diverse population.

Again, I will start with a few facts from our history. I encourage you to fact check the information that is included, research on your own, and continue this conversation with family and friends.

My goal is to continue an important conversation, leading up to the celebration and commemoration of America's Semiquincentennial. I want to help America to fulfill her promises of liberty, equal rights, and protection under "the law of the land." I begin this journey by trying to promote America's unrelenting efforts to unite her diverse citizenry.

This cannot be a burden for any one group. It is the work of many to make this dream a reality. It is a journey with a clearcut destination to promote freedom, liberation, and unity, in mind, in spite of our past.

> *We, as Americans of all races and colors, can continue to draw inspiration and comfort from our faith of our ancestors. Each of us is responsible for doing something about our country…it's up to us to do something positive about our situation here and now… We've got to wake up and make this the greatest country in the world.*
>
> **- Opal Lee**

ALL ABOARD! EVERYBODY'S HELP IS NEEDED!

As we approach the 250th birthday of our relatively new nation's Semiquincentennial, let's prepare to celebrate and commemorate the lives of our Black and White American heroes and sheroes who fought so hard to rid America of this menace called racism. We can also pass their tactics of working together, in unity, Blacks and Whites, to enable others who are still in the struggle. Racism is a sin that we suspect will continue down through the generations, just as other sins continue to do so. Our efforts to diminish its hold are worth it if we can help alleviate its sinful force on some. We, as faith-based Believers, still have hope that, together, we can make a difference. Nothing worthy is to be gained from lies, erasures, or abandonment. We must always take a stand against hate.

Together, our Black and White ancestors helped to bring America to this place, at this time. I believe our ancestors and founding fathers would have been proud of these Americans.

THE PLAN OF ACTION FOR THIS PROJECT

Part 1 introduces *CHOSEN VESSELS: PROMOTING THE UNITY OF AMERICA'S PROMISES BEFORE THE SEMIQUINCENTENNIAL*. I started our project by sharing and exploring a bit of historical information passed down through schooling, informally or formally. Chapters 1-14 consist of lived experiences and real life "learnings." Quotes, discussions, conversations, primary firsthand and researched sources to dialogue about the realities of racism in America are shared. Its purpose is to establish a foundation and premise from our point of references and backgrounds as "seasoned" proud African American faith-based citizens.

Part 2 includes vignettes of brief information about some of America's influential Black and White heroes and sheroes who tried to work boldly toward racial dignity and harmony, over two hundred years ago. That is correct, even during slavery times, these personalities fought valiantly and bravely against the dehumanizing, cruel, and sinful institution of slavery and its existence in America. They fought together, for unity and dignity of all races. They fought against hate.

Part 3 continues with more vignettes about Black and White Americans' heroic attempts to unite and erase provisions for racial abuse and disharmony conducted during the period of post slavery. The Reconstruction era, Jim Crow laws, and Civil Rights Movement battles were fought by these fearless and courageous Americans. They tried to move America toward freedom and equal rights, as promised in the Constitution and other legal documents, to all.

Part 4 offers a summary and a conclusive statement to encourage young American citizens to continue to press forward in the fight against hatred, violence, and divisiveness. All parts of this project are designed to encourage, uplift, and prompt further civil discussions, continuous positive dialogue, and with respect. We encourage and promote these encounters from a fresh and faith-based perspective. This work is dedicated to our talented precious young scholars and their friends of all colors and races.

PART 1

Chosen Vessels:
Promoting The Unity of America's Promises
Before the Semiquincentennial

**A BIT OF HISTORICAL LIVED AND
SHARED EXPERIENCES AND
BACKGOUND INFORMATION**

*To Our Dear Young, African American Scholars,
Let's Discuss The Following Topics*

CHAPTER 1

America, Our Great Inheritance

Like most American ancestors, we, African Americans, inherited this great nation we call America. Some of our inheritances and histories are more unique than others, but it is ours and we hold it in reverence.

Our goal is to begin another intentional project to help our country move toward its worth and value of greatness among her citizens and as a world leader. In spite of adversities, we think of ourselves as chosen vessels with the purpose of unifying and making America a beacon of light in a dark troubled world. Intentionally teaching and promoting togetherness and unity is our purpose and goal for now, through our semiquincentennial in 2026, and fast forwarding for the next 250 years, the quincentennial. The uniting of America's people of all races and colors has to take center stage if we intend to continue our democracy. Future generations are depending on present-day outcomes and decisions.

Past American heroes and sheroes that are introduced and re-introduced in this content, have been outstanding fearless advocates, activists, abolitionists, and American role models. They unselfishly defined, practiced, demonstrated, and sacrificed for their beloved country and nation, the United States of America. We can make this our major goal as modern-day citizens, as well. We must teach the truth about our goals, motives, purposes, and intent as a great nation of diverse Americans. We can do that and so can you.

As a retired educator, I want to continue promoting this type of unity in and for America. I want to keep using my life and faith-based resources in an effort to teach love, unity, and hope. I want to encourage all of our American citizens to focus on the beauty and value of our country, physically and geographically, as well. When we value it, we will take better care of it. But, above all, let's celebrate the vast array of peoples, of all races, colors, ages, religions, cultures, ethnicities, and nationalities. That is the idea America promotes! It makes our country so unique and special. There is so much need and room to spread love, hope, and "life abundantly."

I want all citizens of these United States, however, to feel honored and privileged for their connectedness and status as Americans. They each must feel a sense of pride and belonging. Then, they, in turn, can share it with their fellow and future Americans. Hate and divisiveness will not have a home in these United States of America.

While nothing on earth is utopia, we can and must continue to aim for the absolute best. That will not come in teaching hatred and divisiveness. Our goal is to encourage freedom, liberty, equality, and unity …I want to promote togetherness. When certain plans, actions and laws are in place and enacted upon, I firmly believe that "if you can teach one, you can teach the other."

Again, it is a challenge with so many different races, groups, and ethnicities, but it is not impossible. It is a blessing and an opportunity. It gives focused purpose to our lives as faith-based Believers. It is worth the effort to continue to strive to keep these United States of

America as free of hatred, animosity, racism, bigotry, and other mean-spirited hurtful and sinful deeds, as possible. It is about America, our home, our country, and God's purpose in our lives.

I suspect that I don't know all of the answers, yet. But I have been blessed to have lived for many years. I have a multitude of positive 'lived and learned' experiences to share from my past. My faith and some wonderful triumphal victories have helped me to overcome feelings of hatred for other Americans, due to their race and the color of their skin. I have witnessed much, and yes, I feel confident in saying that I know some of the answers. Age, in jest, would have me to think I know most, or all, of the answers to fighting racist un-American behavior. Common sense, on the other hand, begs to differ. Seriously, I want to share my thoughts over the many years on my journey as a faith-based, eighty-year-old proud African American female, who knows personally, helpful ideas about 'rising above racism' and hatred and continuing to move forward.

I offer it from my perspective and context of the world in which I have lived, learned, and loved, during parts of these two centuries.

My beliefs are begotten from my background of experiences and may very well differ from others; but that is okay with me, and I hope it will be okay with you. We can always agree to disagree. I encourage you, the reader, regardless of your age, race, religion, or other distinguishable features, if you are an American, let's focus on uniting. It's best for America. Together, we can rid or diminish America's shameful, embarrassing, and hurtful roles some of her people have shown in making a mockery of "our land of freedom, liberty, and equality for all."

OUR BLACK AND WHITE AMERICAN UNFINISHED PROJECT

Actually, together, our Black and White ancestors began this project, over two hundred years ago. We must continue its goal for our diverse countrymen, our freedom, and future generations to celebrate the uniting of the states of America.

Together, Black and White Americans and other races, I believe, can make it happen. We can teach our future generations the rationale to move beyond hate in this diverse country. The song, "You've Got to Be Carefully Taught," written in 1949, is apropos today. It is an award-winning musical for many reasons. "South Pacific," by Rodgers and Hammerstein, carries a strong message on the idiocy of hate. This song's lyrics consist of clear-cut down to earth comments on ways hatred, bigotry, and prejudices are taught and preserved. It's simple, easy to follow, and it's true. It highlights how flimsy negative, and divisive attitudes and prejudicial ideas are learned and passed down from generation to generation. It is a classic and powerful statement against racism and divisiveness.

I intend to use a similar methodology to teach the opposite. In 1949, when this song was written, Jacksonville, Texas, my hometown, would not have allowed me the freedom or opportunity to watch this musical. If I had been able to view it, it would have been done in a separate space or place. Why? *Think about it.* Were they afraid I would have torn the seats? Smacked on my food too loudly? Dirtied up the place? No! I was Black, and this was the way most of America, formally and informally, taught us (Black and White) to hate… thru divisiveness and a lack of respect for other cultures and races.

Thank God that America has changed and matured over the last few years in some respects. She examined how some citizens were being discriminated against, and respected the wishes of fellow Americans, Black and White, who opposed this treatment of fellow citizens.

They wanted to obey the laws and ideas of our new world and make changes. However, another great piece of work comes to mind, by Robert Frost, "We have miles to go before we sleep." In other words, there is much work left in America's "unfinished project," the Emancipation. But I believe the freedom and equality America promised to all of our ancestors, is worth continuing the effort and goals.

Let's visit these lyrics and continuously think of positive ways to make our 'great' country even greater for all of her citizens…

"YOU MUST BE CAREFULLY TAUGHT…!"
by Richard Rodgers II and Oscar Hammerstein

You've got to be taught to hate and fear,
You've got to be taught from year to year,
It's got to be drummed in your dear little ear—
You've got to be carefully taught!

You've got to be taught to be afraid.
Of people whose eyes are oddly made,
And people whose skin is a different shade—
You've got to be carefully taught.

You've got to be taught before it's too late,
Before you are six or seven or eight,
To hate all the people your relatives hate—
You've got to be carefully taught!

I don't promote racism and bigotry. I am too proud and too blessed! The purpose of my work is to teach the opposite of hate and divisiveness due to race and skin color. I am a freedom-loving American who, like many others, strives to teach our faith-based youth for now and the next generations. My time, as an 80- year-old, is much too valuable! I believe yours, no matter what the years, is as well!

Let's begin the challenges of using these lyrics to "rise and build!" and intentionally begin (or continue) to teach Americans NOT TO HATE. ... I offer it from my perspective and context of the world in which we have lived and loved during these two centuries.

CHAPTER 2

A Brief Look at America's Major Problem Through My Lens

In celebration and commemoration of the United States' upcoming Semiquincentennial, we, as Americans of all races and colors, can draw inspiration from the struggles and successes of our Black and White founders and ancestors. The work needed to achieve the level of expectations of our founding population, however, is an "unfinished project." From its inception, America knew there were serious flaws, missteps, and misdeeds exercised in the formation of "our new" nation. But there was always hope.

I believe one of its most glaring and most challenging misdeeds had to do with the proper handling of multiple races, colors, and cultures of its diverse inhabitants. This brought about the need for many acceptable choices and wise decisions that had to be made. Since America was conceived by the founders as a free, fair, faith-based country, the system of government, over these groups, had to reflect this in some manner. I believe, our wise ancestry scrutinized fairly and seriously and knew that dire, crucial, and moral changes had to be established to continue as a country of "liberty and goodwill to all." There were so many of us who did not look alike, nor did we

15

speak the same common language. That task is still being dealt with as we approach 250 years.

America has forged ahead in her role as a world leader in materialistic comforts, military power, space travel, education, and medical research, digital and modern-day technologies, and many more new and innovative accomplishments… possibly beyond our forefathers' wildest dreams. However, the majority of discomforts, disappointment, and divisiveness in our country, as we approach this historical milestone, the 2026 Semiquincentennial, centers around one major topic of dire concern… racism. Of course, there are other pressing matters and issues (climate change, poverty, immigration, health care, economy, etc.), but forms and hints of racism have always been present in these issues, as well.

I contend that a major reason racism is so prevalent and has been around so long is its "proximity." In a multicultural society, such as is evident, proudly so, in America, the specimen is always present. The major human prey on which racism feeds are easily visible targets, as an individual or group, for hatred and divisiveness. It takes very little thought, if any, to participate in this type of behavior. You can just look at a person that might be different from you in appearance and decide, *I am not supposed to like that individual or group. I don't need to know about his "character" or values. I see his color. And I must let my children know, so that they, too, can let their children know," …blah, blah, ad nauseum.*

Americans of all races and colors are limiting wonderful life experiences and social opportunities when they decide to give in to feelings of dislike and hatred due to skin color or racial differences. Try the opposite. Let me count the ways: How should I love others? As my brother! As my friend! As my neighbor! As my fellow American!

Other targeted populations and topics demanding our nation's time: Sexism, Gender Equity, climate control, illegal drugs, Border control, domestic terrorism, poverty, etc., take a little more effort, and perhaps, educational assessment and skills.   Racism? Nope. I see you. Bam! It's done. My father, my grandfather, his father's grandfather, etc., taught us to hate "them"!

Maybe it will take a "rocket 'AI' scientist" to figure it out, but I, as a faith-based octogenarian, feel like I can offer some practical lived advice regarding a dangerous secretive enemy that has been amongst us, dividing us, for over 250 years… racism. It continues to be a dangerous and threatening force to our democracy. While the other categories mentioned are marginalized and problematic for a great number of our citizenry, racism surpasses, supersedes, and stands out over the rest. It is more thorough, convenient, and customizable, due mainly to its easy-to-target factor, skin color, and racial identity.

CHECKING TWO BOXES: RACE AND GENDER

Race and skin color is an ever-present target that even if you wanted to do so, you can't hide easily. Sexism and gender are close due to the same visibility factors. And I want to hurriedly add, "women should not be treated as second class citizens in America due to feminism alone." Our country's Constitution does not support, embrace, or condone that type of reasoning and practice. But as an eighty-year-old citizen who grew up "checking two of the boxes" of the two, Black and female, I am in a position to compare, fairly. Trust me. One is worse (racism) than the other and has been so, for many reasons and many years.   Remember too, when the 19th Amendment was passed giving White women the right to vote, that did not give Black women that same right. Black women were still denied that right until about three decades later. Race and gender mattered in this situation as it has in others. Racism and sexism have never been the same.

The enactment of laws to regulate actions manifested as a result of this hidden and open sin is ongoing and, seemingly, must prevail. We must continue to work to unite America by eliminating the acceptance, tolerance, and support for racism in our nation. Racism, overtly and covertly, divides our country and aborts its greatness. It does not represent our democracy. It does not belong here in our diverse population of America. We must see it as a dreadful sin and an immoral act that is anti-faith-based and anti-American. We, working together, Black Americans and White Americans, must continue to unite forces for the good of the nation.

Our forefathers put forth powerful struggles and admirable fights in an effort to build our country and make it free of hostilities and practices of racism, even in the days of slavery. These United States of America have been truly blessed over the years, in spite of her flaws. We cannot allow its demise under our watch because we did not put forth a concerted intentional effort to try to stamp it out. We must continue to fight against any divisive and deadly evil domestic forces that will destroy our democracy. Sometimes, little by little, huge powerful governments are destroyed unsuspectingly. The constant immature name-calling, nit picking, personal attacks, mimicking, political polarization, and infighting must stop! We can proceed and succeed as a superpower if we avoid destroying ourselves from within. The destruction of our democracy in this manner is as real as from outside foreign enemies. America looks weak and vulnerable when we are warring against each other. We must become more united. The United States must be the world's role model in this effort. "Each of us is responsible for doing something about our country…it's up to us to do something positive about our situation in America. There is no denying that we must continue to unite and work together…" is an admonishment of Dr. Opal Lee, the grandmother of Juneteenth. "We've got to wake up and make this the greatest country in the world."

I, an octogenarian, believe that when more inclusive and united strides toward this effort happens, these United States of America will stand taller and stronger. It will become even more productive and admired by other peoples of the world. Perhaps more importantly, *her own people* will remain committed, patriotic, and honor and admire her more! There will be little room for entertaining the idea of insurrections, successions, protests, sit-ins and other, divisive (but needed if peaceful) hostile demonstrations against a just and equitable government. It is when our nation will look its best! Very few will have to point out, verbally or on paper, how great our country is for its diverse population and people. We all will know! We will live it!

A CAUSE FOR CELEBRATION!

So, as we approach the 2026 celebrations, my hope is that we realize, in spite of adversities, our democracy stands out as a workable and worthy experiment. But the Federal, state, and local laws and protection must be enforced equitably and fairly throughout this diverse land.

I believe that the framers of the United States Constitution were wise and blessed in writing a document to build a solid foundation for a strong and diverse nation. It is labeled as the most important governing document in the United States of America. It protects our individual rights and liberties, regardless of our race and gender. We just need the "overseers, Black and White, politicians, and leaders to enforce the 'laws of the land'" equitably.

For over 250 years we have longed for the promises of true emancipation to be enforced in our diverse communities. Now, we need wise and blessed men and women to enforce the most powerful document, the law of the Land, our United States Constitution, equally and equitably across the land. Each of the writers knew that the population of America would likely continue as it appeared at the time of the drafting and writing. Surely persons as wise as the framers of the Constitution would not have ignored such a versatile and diverse population. *Would they?* I don't think so. I think the writers wanted to include every citizen, no matter what race was present, and those who came later as Americans. If they were citizens, they were included. Our country's population, from its inception, consisted mainly of Blacks, Whites, Mexicans, and Native Americans according to early census data. Our founding fathers and our ancestors came to America for many different reasons and under many different circumstances. Remember, too, some were already here. However, I believe the Constitution was not written with any of these reasons or circumstances in mind, specifically. It was for us who are recognized as citizens and who accept the responsibility of citizenship in this great country.

I believe, as an African American, that "we didn't ask to come here, but we are here… and we are glad about it." Many other Americans did not come under similar circumstances. They just wanted very badly to become American and partake of its vast number of resources and opportunities. They wanted jobs, education, and opportunities to reach personal goals. Some came seeking asylum, religious freedom, or seeking refuge from persecution… Whatever the reasons, most of us love and respect America as our home, and as a powerful and significant inheritance from our past. Either way, we feel we belong here. It is a great nation built with the help of our ancestors. They contributed human and financial sacrifices to make this a powerful country. We must respect and honor them for that. We can and must allow ourselves the right to enjoy it.

With the Constitution as the foundation of its political and governing system, America has attempted to put into place an ideal effort to manage its huge and diverse population of citizens. Its purpose still is to provide guaranteed rights to all United States citizens regardless of who they are in the population. It is not perfect and was written by imperfect men. I believe; however, it is primarily built on faith-based values and principles. It is unique, inclusive, and it is ours. If you are an American citizen, these are promises and expectations on which we, anti-slavery constitutionalists, activists, abolitionists, and faith-based Believers can depend.

OTHER IMPORTANT DOCUMENTS AND LAWS HAVE BEEN ADDED...

These and additional documents have played a significant role in shaping American democracy and governance. They have helped to protect individual rights and liberties, promote freedom and democracy, and ensure that all Americans are treated equally under the law. When these promises are kept and laws and rights are enforced equally amongst its citizens, we have cause for celebration!

Name something you learned in this chapter to help you not to hate other Americans, regardless of their color.

____

____

____

____

CHAPTER 3

No Desire to Hate, Many Reasons to Love

Retired educator, faith-based Civil Rights Activist and Juneteenth advocate, Dr. Opal Lee, stated in one of her many speeches that "if you can teach people to hate, you can teach them to love." Dr. Lee meant those words in spite of racial incidents and heartbreaking experiences in her past. From seeing her family's home burned to the ground by people who did not want Blacks in "their" neighborhood, to other incidents witnessed over her years of becoming a nonagenarian Civil Rights Activist, faith-based leader, and human rights advocate. She declares, "there is no desire to hate. Besides, just who exactly are you going to hate? Not every white person was a part of that mob that burned our home, were they? However, every part of the mob was white."

Seriously, we couldn't start hating on other folks just because they were White…that would have made me a racist, and I can think of too many more things I'd rather be in this world, than a racist.

Consciously or unconsciously, in living our daily lives, we can all accomplish this same task and attitude of accepting or rejecting others based upon the majority of interactions we have experienced with them. Never just because they do not look like us or who may not have our same skin color; but it must come from the heart that is fueled by a Supreme Being. To forgive and/or to forget tragic, traumatic, evil acts directed at you (or someone you love) caused by something you have no control over (skin color or racial traits) calls for help from a higher Being. It must happen from within…you must have a faith-based connection to see the light under the darkness of this humongous sin, racism.

I believe, beyond a shadow of doubt, that racism is a despicable sin. There should not be a place for it in America. Each of us must do our part to reduce or get rid of it on our watch. It should not be "someone else's problem."

If you are an American, regardless of color, we all need to do something! I believe WE all CAN do something…"

1) Speak a kind word or thought to a person of another color.

2) Judge others by their character, not "their group" or what you "heard."

3) Offer helpful tips, compliments, suggestions, and constructive critiques.

4) Provide a "for real" smile, an honest and sincere prayer for their well-being, and

5) Every now and then engage in "a casual conversation about our Creator's purpose for each of our lives."

Believe it or not, over the years, I have found the use for one or more of this type of actions and behaviors to be helpful in eliminating racist beliefs, negative thoughts, opinions, and other deceptive and divisive forces of evil, hatred, and racism! There is nothing mystical about this approach. Its purpose is to bring people together while seeing their real humanity.

WORKING TOGETHER AND UP CLOSE DESTROYS MYTHS

Working together and up close destroys myths and beliefs and feelings of inferiority as well as superiority. Many of our Black and White American youth were taught informally that they were less than or greater than other Americans. When America thrived on segregation and separation of the races, there was little chances of changing that mindset. When laws and opportunities they afforded made it possible for all Americans to interact up close, many myths between the races were demolished. Those schools that allowed the Ruby Bridges, the James Meridiths, and many other "first Blacks to enroll," watched in awe. We discovered the many ways God's creatures were alike! We only thought we were different!

Whether in sports, recreation, entertainment, schooling, nurturing, and sharing the good times, or mourning through bad times, as Americans (of all races) we are much more alike than we are different.

For me, this became very evident as a result of various careers over the years. As a teacher in classrooms of children of all races and ages; K- College levels, many, many similarities existed. It became very clear that if you could not visibly see the colors represented, you would never be able to distinguish which was which. Some students were highly motivated and wanted to excel in every class. Some students of all races were lazy, late, and "laidback." Some were social "butterflies" and popular. Suffice it to say, not all of any one race could sing, dance, play basketball or work math and physic equations. They all forgot their lunches, lessons, and manners, occasionally. Depending on age, all races wanted to talk about what was going on in their homes and amongst their parents, if you wanted to hear. Nothing was too "bad" to share. Trust me, many of the feelings of inferiority were debased when I had the opportunity to work with my White colleagues. Feelings of distrust, suspicions, and other uncomfortable situations and thoughts were dismissed from my outlook on life; and they disappeared as a result of working together and up close with my fellow Americans.

My background included teaching and supervising staff at the Junior and Senior college levels as well. Same scenario. I experienced the good, the bad, and the ugly amongst the employees. Black and White 'haters' must move beyond hatred due to this thing about skin color! It is a "laborious artificial point of reference!" We must move beyond monolithic and stereotypical labels, ideas, and unfounded thinking. Again, we are much more alike than we are different. When huge noticeable differences occurred, it was much more likely to be dictated by financial standings or levels of poverty. Both, of course, were present in all of my career and classroom settings, regardless of my subordinates, parents, students' races, or skin color.

I want to intentionally interject that poverty is worse in many, many respects than racism. That is, of course, another book; but trust my wisdom on that, as well. Again, I know both. And thank God, in America, you can avoid one when you are paid wages for your worth… poverty.

Some of our founding fathers and ancestors, Black and White, always had the foresight to visualize and hope for unity in America. Why would they have chosen hatred and racism as a way to move the nation forward? Over the years, under various and diverse circumstances, we have demonstrated some degrees of success in working together as Americans. We must share this emphasis in our teachings to young scholars against hate. We have shown some of what our ancestors believed we could accomplish over these last 250 years while living in an imperfect society. Without the pressures of racism weighing our society down, much more could have been accomplished. But I am a proud Americans, whose goal is to make others proud, as well.

THE MILITARY EXPERIENCE IN TEACHING AGAINST HATE

As far back as I can remember, or research, there have been many attempts for some Blacks and Whites to work together, in unity, to build a stronger America. The military, even in the days of the Revolutionary War and slavery times, was one of the first institutions to embrace members of our multicultural and multiracial population. Leading White Americans did this because we could be an asset and of value to them, outside of slavery. They always knew that we were capable of doing what any other human was capable of doing, beyond being assigned the duty of being a slave in the fields. So, they offered a deal to Black people, "you help us win this war, and we will help you earn your freedom. If you come and join us in the Union Army, we will extend emancipation rights to you." *All of a sudden, value was placed on African Americans, which was not there totally when they were enslaved!*

Since that time in history, some of the most celebrated acts of unity between the races have been those born and developed in the military. Those acts of togetherness mandated under those circumstances, taught many Americans how to overcome hate for each other. When our Armed forces united to defend our country against Foreign Wars and regimes of other countries, we were there, together. America's enemies became the enemies of all of her citizens, regardless of race, color, or creed. Racism, skin color, and feelings of superiority were still present among some of the troops. However, high-ranking military officers began to slowly rid traces of overt segregation and racism themselves. They witnessed the valor and the value of unity amongst the Black and White military men and, finally, women. This new respect, slowly, but surely, trickled down to others under their command. You can look toward leadership in your fight against racism and divisiveness. If it is not evident there, the struggle is even greater. Real change in behavior against hate should come from the top down. It has always been a help in teaching Americans, in a diverse nation, against hate.

TRUE PATRIOTISM AND DETERMINATION NOT TO HATE

Even though our foreign enemies could eat and use facilities that our brave dedicated Black soldiers could not use, they fought anyway. We fought together in every branch of the Armed services. We have taken advantage of being included and integrated into America's efforts to build a united safe society, wherever we were needed. Historically, our roles were seen as messmen or menial, but they were essential in helping America to function and win the wars. Being free of hatred and racism helped us to be able to get along and show support for each other whenever opportunities were offered.

I had many family members who were military veterans. Almost every service member was held in high esteem upon their returns home. In our churches and community events special recognition was a big thing in our little East Texas towns amongst the old Blackjack community, near Troup, Texas. Even though most of us did not know the "enemy," we understood who we were fighting for…our country, America!

"SHOULD I SACRIFICE TO LIVE 'HALF AMERICAN?'"
- JAMES G. THOMPSON, 1942

Perhaps one of the most challenging, and telling, situations that haunted America's conscience was the hypocrisy evidenced by our nation toward its Black recruits. This renown letter was published in the Pittsburg Courier the year I was born, in 1942. It was filled with thought provoking questions. Many Blacks and some Whites waited with bated breath to hear the answers. Thompson, like many young men of that day, was troubled and concerned about the enemy abroad as well as the "one within." But notice the love for America expressed despite the acknowledgement and challenges of adversity… Hope and Faith are evident in his expressions. Patriotism is evident in his expressions. This is another way to teach against hate. Here are excerpts to read and consider before further discussions…

"Like all true Americans, my greatest desire at this time, this crucial point of our history is a desire for a complete victory over the forces of evil, which threaten our existence today. Behind that desire is also a desire to serve, this, my country, in the most advantageous way. Most of our leaders are suggesting that we sacrifice every other ambition to the paramount one, victory. With this, I agree; but I also wonder if another victory could not be achieved at the same time. After all, the things that beset the world now are basically the same things which upset the equilibrium of nations internally, states, counties, cities, homes, and even the individual."

"Being an American of dark complexion and some 26 years, these questions flash through my mind: *Should I sacrifice my life to live half American? Will things be better for the next generation in the peace to follow? Would it be demanding too much to demand full citizenship rights in exchange for the sacrificing of my life? Is the kind of America I know worth defending? Will America be a true and pure democracy after this war? Will colored Americans suffer still the indignities that have been heaped upon them in the past?"*

"These and other questions need answering; I want to know, and I believe every colored American, who is thinking, wants to know. I suggest that while we keep defense and victory in the forefront that we do not lose sight of our fight for true democracy at home. The "V for Victory" sign is being displayed prominently in all so-called democratic countries, which are fighting for victory over aggression, slavery, and tyranny. If this V sign means that to those now engaged in this great conflict, then let colored Americans adopt the double VV for a double victory: The first V for victory over our enemies from without. The second V for victory over our enemies within. For surely those who perpetrate these ugly prejudices here are seeking to destroy our democratic form of government just as surely as the Axis forces."

"In way of an answer to the foregoing questions in a preceding paragraph, I might say that there is no doubt that this country is worth defending; things will be different for the next generation; colored Americans will come into their own, and America will eventually become the true democracy it was designed to be. These things will become a reality in time; but not through any relaxation of the efforts to secure them."

"In conclusion let me say that though these questions often permeate my mind, I love Americans and am willing to die for the America I know will someday become a reality."

The following week, the paper announced that it had published the insignia, The Double V, "to test the response and popularity of such a slogan+ with their readers. The response had been overwhelmingly supportive. All realized the need for victory over our enemies on the battlefields abroad and the continuous fight for freedom we waged against our enslavers at home. The "Double V Campaign" continued.

It helped to bring about change in the governing of a diverse American population. On July 26, 1948, President Harry Truman issued Executive Order 9981, which ordered the desegregation of the U.S. Armed Forces. The military service of Black men and women before and after the desegregation order, and the strength of the Double V Campaign, helped to inspire the modern Civil Rights Movement that began in earnest just after the war ended. This executive order brought Americans together upfront and up close enough to discover each other. Both efforts remain worthy efforts to teach against hate and division in our country.

AFFIRMATIVE ACTION REASONING IN TEACHING UNITY

Fortunately, or unfortunately, our opportunities to teach love and not to hate, were mandated by laws in most cases. We saw the initial inclusion into the military as being a needed demonstration against hatred and separatism. Some might say, it was our ancestors' way of helping to "teach us how to love." These founding examples and principles forced us to see each other as fellow creations of the same Maker. The major purposes of our Constitution and other governing acts and documents were to create freedom, unity, and harmony among the diverse populations in our country. In other words, we were forced to "work, play, learn, as well as fight," together. These were all lessons that we could not have learned by being separated and isolated from each other. We needed to learn them together. So, our founding fathers were wise to try to implement ways that America could continue to grow and thrive, united, or as "we the people." I believe that these documents and laws are still needed today to encourage togetherness in a diverse nation such as ours.

Affirmative Action was one such document to bring diverse citizens together. I believe Affirmative Action was a great policy that tried to promote diversity and inclusion. It was an attempt to close gaps that had been inaccessible to many Black Americans who wanted to improve their lot in life. They had been denied opportunities that other Americans had enjoyed for generations. The accusations of 'reversed discrimination' are not new in a racist society. It has been used in the past just as successfully. Most Americans, White and Black, know her record has shown that our country has not been equal and fair in sharing resources for all citizens leading up to our Semiquincentennial celebration or commemoration. America (realizing her promises to her diverse population), in turn, will try to correct this blunder only to be bamboozled by citizens who conveniently and carefully construct accusations of "reversed discrimination." When they, in turn, were receiving all of these benefits as chosen citizens, which they were not being discriminated "for" (or they did not see it this way). Why America feels "guilty" enough to abandon ship, we are not smart enough to reason. Maybe someone of your generation can figure it out.

Other goals were substituted to provide equal opportunities in our diverse society. America knows that it needs help in recruiting and advancing qualified minorities, women, persons with disabilities, veterans, and a few other marginalized groups. The enforcement of certain laws is needed to promote diversity and inclusion in the workforce and in other places. Affirmative Action types of programs help to build opportunities for togetherness and working in unity, up close, to become a reality. Only through these programs will some environments ever extend opportunities to one or more diverse citizens. When programs like Affirmative Action happen, it helps American citizens to come together for the good of our nation. They get to know each other from personal interactions, without stereotyping, and prejudging, gathered through the fear of the unknown. Many times, this, inadvertently, reduces the need for hate, and encourages unity amongst fellow Americans citizens who look for an opportunity to make our country more inclusive.

Name something you learned in this chapter to help you not to hate other Americans, regardless of their color.

____

____

____

CHAPTER 4

The Talk! Our Cousin is a Policeman; Our Friends Are Criminal Justice Majors; No, We Don't Hate Law Enforcement

When I was in the classrooms, before retirement, on certain days I invited people from various professions to come in and speak to my classes. I usually called this "Career Day." This was always a special treat for our kids, regardless of their ages. To prepare them, I discussed some of the professions ahead of time. Needless to say, all of the professions were interesting, but some inevitably created more excitement. The law enforcement sessions were most amusing. Everyone had a story to tell. Most were supportive, but many were not. I never detected "hate" for our visiting policemen guests. Most were White males… more curiosity than fear or any other emotion was expressed.

As an older American, I appreciate and depend on law enforcement now even more than when I was much younger. I never hated law enforcement and thought mostly about how cute our friends and relatives were in their uniforms. Granted, I, foolishly and carelessly, did not consider the dangers many of them faced in their jobs every day. But no serious conversation is complete when discussing the manifestation of racism in America without, "the talk."

As a mother, grandmother, and great grandmother, I believe every Black parent should speak to their youth about racist police officers. They must be candid and teach them against hate. With everything they witness in real life and on the news media, it is a difficult, but necessary duty and responsibility. Every wise parent should speak the code or language that is involved. It is on every caring adult's agenda. It is as American as "apple pie." It is our history, from the days of slavery when the first police forces were hired. And, as in other professions and careers, not every applicant and hiree are suitable for the job. The ones who aren't make others look bad. A job of this caliber should never take on just any applicant. It is too special and should only include the best. It is very needed and deserves a special place in a diverse society such as ours.

OVER THE YEARS, WE HAVE BEEN BLESSED TO HAVE LAW ENFORCEMENT

In spite of this, many reputable law enforcement officers have saved many lives, on the streets, in homeless camps, and other places. They have birthed babies in squad cars. They have been role models and mentors for many lost and troubled juveniles. Many, many times these officers have served nobly. (I know because some of them were my cousins, brothers, etc.) But the American history of law enforcement in multiracial environments has been shameful, harmful, and deadly. It is un-American to ignore it and not try to make it better for all the citizens of these uniting states. I do not pretend this fact has not been reality for many people of color in our country during its existence.

DO YOU KNOW WHY LAW ENFORCEMENT WAS FIRST ESTABLISHED IN AMERICA?

Probably like me, you never had really given it a lot of thought. You don't have to now, but if you research this topic and you think about it, you will understand why this system continues to be at odds with certain communities. African Americans in particular, are targets. They always have been. That does not mean we don't need them or their helpful services in today's society. It does not mean we should not keep seeing this profession as a noble one and keep trying to enter into this field or career. It also helps all communities understand and possibly accept the challenges of not hating this group of "protectors."

When Black people were allowed to become hired as officers, we were eager to seek these opportunities. Operating in volatile situations for law enforcement is a routine and daunting task for many officers. Operating within multiracial and multiethnic volatile situations has to be more challenging when those involved are of opposite races, cultures, and attitudes. I believe both parties deserve respect as citizens and "the talk" must reflect this. However, one must be respected, additionally, because that person is in uniform, is an authority figure, knows the rules, is likely to be of a different race, and legally, is armed with a deadly weapon. And "He is just doing his job to the best of his ability when he stopped you for that offense" is what must be taught. Most of us teach our young that, early on, because we hope that the encounter will be safe.

As African Americans, we have never been able to rely totally on the professionalism of an officer just because they are in uniform. We hope that the officer will be professional, brief, and most of all, "one of the good officers." (We all know that they are out there). We hope and pray that our youth, and all citizens, if and when they are stopped, arrested, or "encountered," are not interfacing with someone who is filled with rage, bigotry, and racism, overtly or covertly. Unfortunately, if we "tell the truth and shame a liar," we personally know many people of color, throughout our history, that such an encounter has happened to, and not just a few times, but over and over again. And, historically, America has held only a very few accountable for the "authority figure's" misdeeds. We hope and pray that our youth are approached by an officer who wants only to correct misbehavior. We hope it is a "uniformed, authority, and professional" who will not be consumed with hatred of persons who might be of a different race or skin color.

THE OTHER IMPORTANT PART OF OUR MESSAGE AGAINST HATE

We must continue to teach our young to be highly respectful, cautious, and responsible as young citizens who are determined to avoid trouble. We must equip them with the language that is best to be used when dealing with people of authority. Not every officer is a racist officer, but there is no denying that they are out there. By all means, we must tell them, too, that many who have chosen this profession are not "out to get them." However, their own personal encounters may suggest otherwise. If you make a mistake in making a wrong move or saying the wrong thing, it could very likely end up being really, really, bad. Our history in America has shown that little or no consequences or equal justice will be meted out to perpetrators in uniform. Whether found guilty (a rare possibility), or not, try to avoid verbal (not to mention, physical confrontation) of any kind. In addition, when incidents occur like these, involving persons of mixed races, the majority race is usually supported by local and state political and community officials and leaders.

Media has been a Godsend in our Black communities all over America. Many times, unequal rights and privileges were captured or demonstrated while using this tool.   "Bad, brutal and deadly policing" is un-American and a serious dilemma, and intentionally or unintentionally, teaches hatred and disrespect among America's diverse populations.

That is sometimes seen as a real challenge for good law enforcement officers and citizens of color in America who do not see the need to hate each other. There is an unhealthy amount of distrust and fear for this group and it's not, unfortunately, just among the "criminal element." Our history shows that for years, there was a lack of equal police protection rendered in many of our communities. *Was this due to racism?* In many instances, the answer is a resounding "yes." Policing, as a profession, was introduced to America to protect Whites and their properties, not so much from each other, but from Black people. That is how many law enforcement officers view their role today. This teaches and reinforces hate.

AFRICAN AMERICANS WANTED THE SAME PROTECTION AS OTHER CITIZENS

I never taught my children, grandchildren, great grands, or any other Americans to disrespect persons in uniform who are doing their jobs. I would teach them to applaud and respect that person. I honor law enforcement as a respectable organization and career choice in the workforce. I appreciate the fact and know that they are charged with a huge responsibility of protecting all citizens from criminal activity, breaking laws, and disturbances. I do believe special training to sensitize certain professionals in authority is a must in teaching how not to hate. This would be true, regardless of race, but certainly in extraordinary and intense volatile emotionally charged situations that an officer might experience. When any citizen who is breaking the law is apprehended or accosted by someone who is, supposedly, assigned to interrupt or abort that act, intense resistance, from one, or both sides, is likely to occur, I understand and support that observation. That is another reason I suggest the need for sensitivity training.

Many times, during this process, the application of choices of defense, resolution, or force used, has been dealt out unequally amongst citizens of color. This can breed controversy and unfortunately, hate. It is an American problem that has existed since slavery times when policing was introduced to protect White people and their properties. The exasperation of tensions between police and other law enforcement agencies in the communities they served most often have not looked like them. Sometimes these tragic misunderstood police interactions have involved both races. Many Americans have been puzzled by law enforcement and police work.

On May 13, police dropped a bomb on a Black radical group, MOVE, as officers tried to evict them from their premises. It is said that the police fired over 9,000 to 10,000 rounds of ammunition into the building before dropping the bomb from a helicopter. A police Commissioner, Gregore J. Sambor, directed the bombing…Then what happened?... And a grand jury in 1988, cleared the African American mayor at the time, W. Wilson Goode, and other top city officials of criminal liability for death and destruction resulting from the operation. Several lives were lost. Six men and women and five children were killed. Hearts were broken, people who allowed and/or committed the despicable act were sorry later… the pain and sorrow lingered. This is embedded in the minds of people who are hurting. It is especially heart-breaking when the victims are not satisfied that anyone is being held accountable. Many times, their loss turns from sorrow to anger, and hatred for others who did, or did not, look like them.

SO, IS THIS "RELATIONSHIP" REAL OR IMAGINED?

Some research has shown that people of color are more likely to be stopped and searched by law enforcement officers than White people, according to a 2019 report by the Public Policy Institute of California. It found that Black Californians are more than twice as likely to be searched as White Californians. The report also found that searches of Black civilians are somewhat less likely to yield contraband and evidence than searches of White civilians. Another study conducted by Stanford University, found that police stopped and searched Black and Latino drivers on the basis of less evidence than used in stopping White drivers, who are searched less often, but are more likely to be found with illegal items . These studies suggest that there is a racial bias in law enforcement stops. These studies are not conclusive and do not represent the entire law enforcement community. As in any career or profession, there are small groups that continue to be a threat to unity needed in our nation. Continued research and reform in this area are definitely needed as we approach the Semiquincentennial.

A CONCLUSION FOR AMERICANS WHO DON'T NEED TO HATE

Historically, we have experienced a cruel misunderstood past. Yet, the overwhelming population of African Americans, indigent whites, and other people of color appreciate and respect law enforcement and count it as a blessing. Over the years, African Americans have learned to acknowledge, appreciate, and accept the good, the bad, and the ugly. Poor Whites and other American citizens of color have been victims of bad policing as well. None of these groups, in spite of adversities, dislike police and law enforcement because of race or skin color. They dislike being misused, abused, and victims of police brutality, due to race, skin color, and status in life. They still join police forces, still major in law enforcement as a career offering, and uphold the laws that are allocated equally. But, no Americans, regardless of race or color, respects or appreciates the racist bigoted acts of aggression afflicted upon their sons, (and daughters), under the umbrella of "law enforcement."

Some of the crime control tactics, and bullying maneuvers, are questionable for White faith-based leaders and citizens as well. Even other, good morally sound, White and Black officers question the use of brutal force sometimes used…and would never agree to allowing it to happen to one of their own. Many try to dissuade violence and hateful behaviors among their fellow officers. Too many, however, remain silent and supportive of their fellow officers. They don't know or do not care that these actions are a blight on their profession, especially now that cameras are, seemingly, everywhere. For some law enforcement officers, not all, it appears to be a license, badge, and a uniform to vent their frustrations on certain audiences. Their unchecked bad behavior can cause hate and divisiveness amongst Americans.

With the enforcement of our Founders' laws of equality for her people, America hovers heads and shoulders over other nations. Enforcement, not just promises, of our laws to protect all citizens, regardless of color, must be America's immediate pressing goal. Nations that are older in years and more established than our own will not stand as majestically as the younger United States! But, our country's laws, promises, and pledges must be respected and enforced equally amongst its citizens, regardless of color. It is, joyfully so, a model for the world to admire and imitate, even at just 250 years! It is a workable system for the overwhelming majority of its citizens to appreciate. People all over the world, as well as in America want to live under these enforced, equitable laws, dreams, freedoms, and opportunities promised to its citizens…at the uniting of these states of America!

Name something you learned in this chapter to help you not to hate other Americans, regardless of their color.

CHAPTER 5

A Force to Unite Against Hate: Learning Our Past Helps Us to Prepare for a Better Future

In our Semiquincentennial year of 2026, we can all be prepared to celebrate America's greatness and her work toward unity. Our Black and White ancestors would have wanted us to do so. All of our ancestors have played significant roles in shaping our country's success. Its history, culture, and identity have been influenced globally as well as nationally by the diverse American human tapestry of cultures. Our Black ancestors have contributed and excelled in sports, music, education, sciences, entertainment, art, and left their footprint on every opportunity extended to them. I remember very vividly when our nation did not place credibility in the thought of a Black American president, vice president, or other powerful political leaders.

We could not enroll in the big universities with many of their teams that are led by Black quarterbacks. Trained heart specialists and surgeons over major medical facilities were not the vision of many racists. Ballerinas and gymnasts performing unimaginable feats to win medals for America's teams here and abroad make our ancestors proud because those were some of the dreams that they had for you once racial barriers were removed. Pilots, space engineers, media technologists, entertainers, and on and on the list can go. All are present and accounted for at global notoriety to the dismay and disappointment of racist thinkers…those who did not want to extend inclusive opportunities to people of color. Now is not the time to lose momentum. It is a time for reflection only to renew our move forward on the ideas and values of this great nation. It is a time to celebrate the idea of opportunities and actions needed to finish the project of building a stronger inclusive equitable and just society.

The United States of America is never going to be perfect, but there is much in our legacy and heritage to celebrate and commemorate. Through faith, the enforcement of laws, and patriotic determination to work toward unification in our multicultural society, many Americans have discovered each other as fellow citizens. Down through the years, the enforcement of certain laws (i.e., integration of schools, public parks, and facilities, eating places) affirmative action, integration, and other civil rights, as citizens would not have come about through "volunteerism." Racism has been woven and embedded so deeply into some of our lives, it dictates our readiness to see and interact with other races, regardless of citizenship, as fellow Americans.

To make complete changes to racist feelings of superiority for one group, will not happen suddenly. We are about to celebrate over 200 years of efforts. Nor is it possible to see the opposite behavior, feelings of inferiority, in everyone else who is not of your race. For some, it will take more time, a greater resolve, and determination. How long a person has felt superior, or inferior, to another human being, due to race or color, sometimes predicts the level of difficulty for the release of this attitude. Starting at my age is a little difficult, but even then, it is possible. People don't have to hate other races.

We believe much of whether or not a person is burdened with hate is by choice. Do not choose to hate. Avoid it, as well as those people who choose to hate. If you feel like bigotry and hatred overwhelm you and you just cannot overcome its demonic grip, try these suggestions in diverse environments or situations.

I suggest you practice overt displays of positive attitudes and mannerisms in diverse situations. These behaviors can justify (or fool) another person into believing that real progress is being made toward acceptance, unity, and togetherness. For those who are often marginalized and maligned due to different, real, and sometimes imaginary obstacles, at that moment, it provides hope. It can provide a sense of acceptance and replace the feelings of not belonging. It can cause Black and White fellow Americans to move beyond hate. Practice sometimes leads to perfection. I believe it is most helpful and there is a place for it in teaching against hate and racism. It can be influential in building a degree of racial harmony and tolerance in diverse groups.

Observing and participating in team sports competitions where teams are made up of diverse participants helps. Global representations, and contests, pageants, spelling bees and similar events have contributed to a deeper appreciation for members of opposite cultures. Sometimes, these rewards might seem to be minor and short lived, but many more have given lasting and lifetime impressions. For a while, reasons for hate are absent. Together, in unity, everyone is valued in most of these situations, and all are held in high esteem and honor, regardless of color. When African American winners (as well as other nationalities) are standing on the podium with the American flag draped around them as the Star-Spangled Banner is being sung, it makes an impact on Black and White citizens who love our country.

When our society, especially our youth who have not been taught to hate, observes this positive camaraderie in multi-racial environments, it helps to make a positive difference. It can provide visual support, a true sense of belonging and acceptance, especially in these strategic places and crowds. It teaches Americans we are on the same team. It gives them the opportunities to work, play, and experience the joy of working together, in uniting this diverse culture. It teaches against hate.

I believe covert changes in racist behaviors must be improved through faith, good will, and determination. In other words, if a person is a racist and he or she keeps it to themselves, it is covered up. This is another way to fight the spread of hate in any society. At least for the moment, no one is hurt by it, except the person who carries the heavy burdensome load of hatred... But that is, of course, a choice the "hater" makes. Everyone is not privy, nor should they be, to this "load" you carry about other races and skin color. The person(s) who is targeted is not harmed, either. They probably don't care because they don't know. Please do them that favor and honor.

While I sympathize and wish no one the extra mental and emotional baggage of hate, for the racist, it should be your burden to bear alone. Don't impose those negative feelings, or actions, on another human being due to their race or color. They did not have anything to do with creating their eyes, skin color, or other distinguishable features that cause you to hate them. Ask and answer this question: Is this type of hate justified? Is it fair? Think about it! On the other hand, if another person displays actions or character that you do not agree with, condone, or like, dispose of it in the same proper manner you deem necessary toward any American citizen.

In other words, again, you are dissatisfied with the action, not the color of their skin or race. That is one of the ways you will learn not to hate, due to race or skin color. It is most important and must come from the heart. Pray mightily for them and yourself. Pray that you can be relieved of this heavy burden.

CERTAIN LAWS, WHEN ENFORCED, ARE USEFUL TO ERASE LONG-STANDING RACIST BELIEFS

Affirmative Action laws, integration of public and private events, fostering and adoptions into families, interracial marriages and relationships, and other displays of the successful mixing and mingling of races, help to rid our nation of generational hate.

Even when our system of government enacted certain laws, like Affirmative Action and desegregation of public supported institutions, our citizenship, reluctantly, obeyed these mandates. We, as a diverse nation, were forced to initiate and examine ways to integrate in most instances. In retrospect, Blacks and Whites, through these regulations learned more about each other than our separation of races ever offered. Our children knew very little about Jim Crow laws that many Black Americans suffered through. Even in military assignments, in fighting a common foreign enemy, many White and Black citizens would not have, willingly or voluntarily, fought together. That is an isolated, but very telling revelation of how insane and moronic racism can be. It has taken time and effort to reach this far in racial improvements in our nation. Providing "forced" job opportunities, allotting more inclusive scholarships and financial aid, handling and integrating housing, and other such affirmative actions and mandates caused Americans to put forth more of an effort to interact together as citizens.

I believe these acts can cause discomforts to those who were not willing to share America's vast resources… some of which were gained on the backs of our ancestors. This sometimes breeds hate amongst both groups of Americans when they do not know their histories. I firmly believe it makes a positive difference when Black and White Americans know the truth about their histories… the good, the bad, and the not so good. Americans must learn their history to become more willing to serve and interact in a diverse population of citizens.

Our Black and White ancestors, even in America's inception, figured out that for America to succeed as a nation, all of her people should be given equal opportunities and treatment. Through no fault of our own, this is a very diverse country, whose founding fathers were determined to form a more just union for all. It has always been, even before Columbus "discovered" America. There were different races, colors, and creeds here from the beginning. Not all Americans of color, in that day, were stolen and brought over on ships, nor did they illegally cross the borders. Some were already here, and I believe it was the desires of our forefathers to include everyone in their governing documents while "forming a more perfect union." Their hopes of building a new and better world were honorable and of value. It would not be one of exclusion and hate and divisiveness from within, but one built on a more solid foundation of unity, hope, and "togetherness" for all of her citizens and diverse population of people.

Did The Founding Fathers include Slaves in The Early US Constitution and Documents? I pondered over the idea and consideration that the Founders excluded slaves and people of color in their earliest documents. I, of course, don't know. The language written in all of the documents during that time did not specify the entitlements of slaves. However, it did not specify women either. We believe they were intended to be included if they were American citizens. When there needed to be focused attention paid on "marginalized groups, Amendments like 13, 14,15, and 19 specified inclusions. Think about it…why would the wise and intelligent faith-based framers of our constitution NOT have intended to do so? What would be the major accomplishment for mandating the omission and separation of persons based on skin color and race? Segregation? Divisive citizenry?

They themselves had just escaped a system they felt was unfair, oppressive, overly burdened, and overly taxing. That might have been damaging to the new image they wanted to project. Could it have been ignorance? Desire for extreme power over another human being? A lack of faith?   No, I believe these men were sagacious and just in their thinking on building a strong new world guided by a constitution that would last through many generations and future years. It included a diverse population. America would be admired as a beacon of hope and a beam of light for her people and the rest of the world. That would not be possible in a divided country. It would not be possible in a nation filled with hate and bigotry against each other due to race and skin colors.

I believe the Constitution was intended to unite and govern all its citizens. When these laws are dealt out equally and fairly, there is very little room for division. There is no room or reason for hate. Even though at that time some of the founders owned slaves, the framers knew it was wrong. They knew it was economically profitable, but within a brief period of time, they dropped this despicable practice. (We all have heard the comparison of it was akin to wealthy drug lords selling their wares to their own people. They "knew the harm they were doing, but some of them were so greedy for economic gain, and selling was easy." Like some of the slave owners, some discontinued this business after a while.)

The Founding fathers and the framers of the Constitution who owned slaves continued the fight to abolish it. So, they set out to write the three most important documents in America in the early years of 1776--1778: First was the separation from the British in the Declaration of Independence, the US Constitution, and the Bill of Rights. All were designed, among other things, to seek and build a country of their own and to unite its people as one freedom-loving country. Their plans did not include writing another burdensome addition to the country's already heavily laden experiences in this new world. They, by now, had truly seen the devastation of sicknesses and diseases, infightings, wars, squabbles with indigenous groups and their own, and other challenges of which a new world had brought forth.

Why, then, would wise men, and the best thinkers, not want to write documents, laws, etc. to place America on a less stressful path? Why wouldn't they try to unite her present resources and her people, rather than separating and taxing them even more?

I think they did not agree on how best it should be done, but they knew a more perfect document would be needed. Should freedom and equality be extended to all or just some? How would the "just some" be chosen? Would race and skin color matter?

I believe, our founding forefathers, intended for all to be a part of building and benefiting from this great freshly organized, but established new nation, America. I believe, without a doubt, that America realized she had to make tough choices and wise decisions in moving forward. She had to rethink and redirect attitudes and lifestyles, and slavery was the major challenge for uniting these new states. Many Americans wanted to let this awful and sinful institution go. They did not want this decadent act of enslavement to become a legal reality. It appeared that only those who wanted more than enough, were morally and spiritually corrupt, ruthless, and bullies who were determined to exclude all people of colors, as citizens. They wanted to continue the enslavement of Black men, Black women, and their children to do their work. They wanted it free.

There was definitely a powerful group who wanted to keep slavery as a part of building their personal wealth. They were determined to forfeit any laws that would lead to the uniting of all races and colors. They disagreed and fought adamantly, to promote separatism of America's efforts to unite her people. A small but powerful and influential wealthy group did not want to extend and spread equal rights, share resources equitably, and respect the dignities of people of color in this new world. So, they kept our ancestors enslaved for centuries. Even though there was opposition, they continued to build generations of wealth for their families at the 'human and financial' sacrifice of our Black enslaved (and 'freed') families.

NEEDED PLANS FOR ESTABLISHING AND ENFORCING, GOVERNING OF AMERICA'S DIVERSE POPULATION

Over the years, due to laws implementing uncomfortable changes for some in our society, we have promoted racist attitudes. Our laws which have not been enforced equally or equitably, have caused even more friction. When that happens, there is a tendency to breed hate and resentment among and within groups. If the groups are distinguishable by skin color or race, racist beliefs form. That is exactly what has happened to create tension, animosity, and divisiveness amongst American citizens. So, now, for certain, we firmly believe the time has come that America must be intentional and deliberate in our teaching, preaching, and reasoning in helping to unite our diverse cultures. We cannot afford to leave this important task to a chance happening. In our freedom-loving democracy, there is definite need to teach civility and respect for all

Americans. We must do everything possible to rid these diverse states in America of seeds of hate and divisiveness. This type of discrimination is a very present threat to our democracy.

Many times, seeds of racism manifest themselves in the form of racist rants, behaviors and overt hostile actions taken against another person just because of skin color. Very early on, elementary age youth notice different diversity traits: skin colors, hair textures, eye shapes or colorings, clothing, etc. We believe they are supposed to be able to observe these distinguishing characteristics of another person. What happens afterwards is a major concern to most caring adults. Will they view this encounter as a positive or as a negative one? Will it promote hate or fight against it? It is a feature they will possess for the rest of their lives. I have these fine qualifiers at my age. Even at my age, I notice the physical differences among people when we first meet or interact with them. What we do not applaud for youth, or anyone else, is placing value, or devaluing, a person based on these visual characteristics and traits, alone. No one, children or grown-ups, as American citizens, should be taught to hate, or love, on these qualities of physical presentations, alone. There are no privileges or take-a-ways for these possessions and decisions. In other words, in America, people are not expected to be judged as good or bad, on the basis of skin color or race.

I wish that to minimize the sting of racism, our young American citizens, especially in our communities, churches, and schools, could deliberately and intentionally be taught the importance of loving God, each other, and our country. I believe this because I realize the severity and the difficulty of this humongous and serious task, when I fight against racism. As a faith-based Believer, I wholeheartedly believe and hold in reverence (Ephesians 6:12), "For we wrestle not against flesh and blood, but against principalities, against powers, against the rulers of the darkness of this world, against spiritual wickedness in high places." I believe racism continues to be, as we approach the Semiquincentennial, one of the major causes of unrest, discord, and disharmony in America. It is a very present threat to our democracy. It weaves its ugly, but powerful, head in every "nook and cranny" of our society. It is a devastating sin that, admittedly, attacks and destroys some, more than others. It is a fight for every freedom loving American citizen.

We must acknowledge this fact and continue to work toward decreasing its existence and eliminating it as a part of our society. Even when we cannot fully eliminate the detriment and hurt, we can empower its targets, our American brothers and sisters of the faith, with more hope, good will, and resilience to overcome. I believe when we fight against acts of racism and hatred, we are fighting for America's survival. We are Chosen Vessels to perform God's will of brotherhood toward others. We are fighting against evil and sinful actions against humanity. We are fighting for the same sense of security our ancestors fought for years ago. Our grandmothers used to sing "We are on the battlefield for our Lord!" It is a continuing struggle and fight. However, to help to save our democracy, it is worth it.

We must aim to help all-American law-abiding citizens, Black and White, to feel self-confident and possess a trusting sense of belonging in America. But this accomplishment will not become a reality for people of color without our nation's keeping its promises to them…not just to Whites and Blacks, but to all citizens. When discriminatory actions are practiced, over an extended period of time, with no attempts to hold anyone accountable, the pain and anger of the victims can easily turn to hate. My purpose is to teach against hate.

AMERICA HAS PROMOTED FAITH-BASED VALUES AND PRINCIPLES IN OUR PAST, WHAT HAPPENED?

I don't know who you "hang out" with, but many of my closest friends, relatives, and co-workers are faith-based Believers. I am not perfect yet, but I am pressing toward that goal. If you are led by Godly principles in your life, you will see and feel a profound sense of triumph, victories, and accomplishments, regardless of whatever happens in the world around you. Faith is a personal belief and acknowledgement and connection to a Higher Power. It is a valuable asset in any life. It is, certainly, another book. America has always promoted Faith-based values and principles. "In God we trust" can be seen throughout early inscriptions, writings in prominent places and documents. Physically, America's clear intentions was to remember God's presence in most of our daily actions. Inscriptions on many federal buildings, monetary exchange; but somehow, the signs and markings are still present, but the spiritual meaning has waned. "God is love" is still a much-needed refrain in our efforts and daily lives to teach against hate.

Most Americans know that inequities and discrimination have existed for centuries in our nations. But our faith, beliefs, and knowledge must be followed up with actions. In your civic and government classes you have probably discussed the 19th amendment. It allowed White women to vote, but not Black women. Racism is much stronger in America than sexism. That is why Black women had to wait almost four decades later to be allowed to vote. Our faith and patriotism have to move us out of our comfort zones to help move our country forward. When attempts are made to legislate and rectify some of these seeds of racism, strong and powerful efforts are made to "roll back the hands of time." These "roll backs" are usually disguised with language like "reversed discrimination." Racist beliefs make such efforts seem like it is okay to make these types of judgement calls. America cannot move forward in such a pattern. It is unfair and it is un-American.

I believe our America must commit to enforcing fair, just, and equal inclusive protection of laws and practices of freedoms. I understand the hurt, anger, disappointment, fear, and that hatred can evolve from these emotions. To change racist attitudes and beliefs, we must move many people way, way, out of their comfort zones. Many have occupied that position of privilege for generations and centuries ago. Many have never shared anything equally. But America is changing too rapidly for racism and comfort to co-exist as it has in the past. America is becoming too diverse to ignore the need to unite and stress the importance of togetherness, E Pluribus unum! But aggressive violent reactions are likely to occur without law and order.

When one group has been privileged and accustomed to being "'first in line' (for centuries) in all of the economic wealth and gain, eating places, entertainment venues, "using the bathrooms," etc.," and now change is on the horizon, is challenging. You are being told that you must share equally with others (who you were taught for generations were inferior to you due to their race and skin color) in line. You will very likely become uncomfortable. Your level of discomfort and the resilience from this ordeal may change to rage, anger, and even hate. Hopefully, that will not be the case. We all must unite and teach, preach, vote, and abide by the Constitution and other laws that teach us to work together and unite America. I believe it can be done. John 3:16 does, as well as many others.

AMERICA "DESERVES" YOU!

I have held many toddlers and little ones during my lifetime. Some were my own and many were not. It is a pleasure to tend to them and observe their socialization skills. Babies and most little ones can love so innocently. They see skin color, but they have not learned to hate, yet. It doesn't matter that their new friend or care giver is Black or White, Brown Yellow or Red…they just know they have fun together. They belong. They matter. "They sometimes squabble, or want the same toy at the same time, but they have not been taught to hate. Their lifestyle has not been hampered by not wanting people of certain colors in their classrooms, or eating in the same restaurant, or living in their neighborhood, or getting a new job, or house, or raise, or promotion, or etc., etc., blah, blah, ad nausea. They do not spend sleepless nights trying to figure out how to demote, or take away some benefits, or deny entry into "their abundant and overflowing' circle of resources and influences, due to race or skin color." Many grown-ups intentionally or unintentionally teach themselves to hate. Then they want others to join them and set out to make it happen. America deserves better. America deserves you. Give her your best. There should be no room for hate in this land of so much.

Like most Believers, as many of our ancestors were, we sometimes feel overwhelmed, alone, and feel like giving up. But, again, as Believers and born of chosen noble ancestry, we continue to move forward. We continue to "rise and build" in this constant struggle to unite as we find a place in our freedom loving nation. Our ancestors' contributions and achievements were special. Their unwavering commitment to America cannot be ignored or blotted from history. Their ideas, values, culture and identities, patience, tolerance, and resiliency are a model for us today.

James Weldon Johnson and other noted clergy encouraged our ancestors in the iconic Black National Anthem, "Lift Every Voice and Sing," to love America in spite of the adversities they faced. Even after slavery, many of our ancestors faced blatant racist behaviors due to their race and Black skin. John Rosamond Johnson, his musically talented brother, set this amazing piece of poetry to music. It was very comforting then, and for many, provides that same level of comfort today. In the book of seminars for young adults, choosing to Lift Every Voice and Sing, the author shares Johnson's empowering lyrics with messages of tenacity, courage, and hope felt by our ancestors, even then. Yet, it is a timeless set of lyrics that are invaluable when dealing with overt and covert racist behavior today.

The author intentionally and purposely included musical activities that were repetitious of the lyrics so as to make sure this special work does not fade away soon. Her intent is to use these Godly and non-toxic lyrics and faith-based seminars to teach against hate… for self as well as others. It is another way of avoiding hate in a racist society when you are the victim. Many of our Black and White ancestors who were pastors and religious leaders, included Johnson's inspirational and motivational work in their church hymnals. Look in your hymnal, it's probably there today! These pastors wanted to use their tools of authority, in religious settings and from the pulpits, to make a difference and to teach against the acceptance of hate and racism, as well.

Early churches in America, the Quakers, Unitarians, Methodist Ministers, and other clergy spoke out, adamantly, against the horrors of slavery, Jim Crow laws, and in the Civil Rights era. Each of these parts of history shows the length, depth, and extent of time we have struggled with racism in this country. America's weaknesses, one she has not overcome yet, has been the inability to overcome greedy, sinful bullies: who were small in number, but very powerful and full of hate. They were in charge and overruled those under them. Our grandparents had a saying, "God sits high, but he sees low." In other words, "Let the wheat and the tares grow together on the day of my coming, I will separate them" (Matthew 13: 24-30).

In other words, I truly believe, God's got it. These words are comforting to Believers. This reduces the will to hate…**so** we must continue to pray and work to move forward.

For those of us who choose to believe that our country was built on Christian and faith-based values, we understand and choose to believe our Creator still cares. That is comforting and provides hope when hateful mean-spirited racist antics and experiences are hurtled your way. I believe (as many of my ancestors did) God pre-destined our "harvest" in America. Let's celebrate! Don't hate! America deserves citizens like you. We are what makes the country great.

Name something you learned in this chapter to help you not to hate other Americans, regardless of their color.

____

____

____

____

____

____

____

____

____

____

CHAPTER 6

Race and Skin Color Can't Devalue Our Human Worth

In our Semiquincentennial year of 2026, we can all be prepared to celebrate America's greatness. Our Black and White ancestors would have wanted us to do so. After all, it is our choice as American citizens. I CHOOSE to value my worth on this planet and more importantly, right here in America. The United States of America is never going to be perfect, but perfection is a goal we should always look for in such a blessed land of plenty. There is much in our legacy and heritage to celebrate, commemorate, and share. Nevertheless, it must be said that there have been huge periods of time over the past 250 years when we did not work together in harmony or united, as one equal opportunity America. We don't want that to ever happen again.

Our Semiquincentennial will mark 250 years of America's Independence from Great Britain. We were two separate human entities or groups then, with one clearly designated and established as being superior to the other. We were divided by skin color and race. This was not just during the period of slavery. It has lasted through the years. Yes, America is the greatest country in the world and is recognized as a superpower, today, as we approach the

Semiquincentennial. But, in America, race has always been of major concern…a sort of 'thorn in the side.' Not always skin color, because for some, even if your skin color was hardly distinguishable from another race, it did not matter. You belonged to a group…a race. Your eyes could be blue, green, or whatever. If you had one drop of "Negro blood" in your blood line (however it was measured, we are unsure), your race was "Negro or Black." As Black Americans, our ancestors were limited in many respects, due to segregation and separation determined by this fact.

WHAT IF TIME HAD BEEN SPENT ON INTEGRATING INSTEAD OF SEGREGATING

Who knows what America could have produced and added to her greatness if "race or skin color" had not been an issue at the "birthing" of this new nation. During this timeframe, if our nation's leaders had made greater use of the time and resources of all natives and inhabitants of this land…think of what this country might have been like today!

The early years during colonial times were rough to say the least. Much time was spent fighting wars and internal conflicts. First, of course, America spent a considerable amount of time, and lives, seeking independence from the British. This had to be done. After receiving this prize, imagine what could have happened if America had taken advantage of the human resources and capital in a positive, friendly, and honorable way. With its newly "discovered human capital," greatness and world dominance as we enter our Semiquincentennial could have very well been a reality. The Blacks, Whites, Mexicans, and Indigenous people who were already here could have contributed, together, so much more to the success of our country! Wars for the possession of more property, the enslavement and possession of more people to work free and control, greed, and the desire for more power were common motivational factors as to why this path was not travelled. There was constant conflict, instead of constant progress and constant agitation, instead of forward movement. Sicknesses and diseases plagued the land. Hatred, distrust, and disunity impeded progress.

Our nation's Colored people and White citizens were divided over issues surrounding the equal acceptance and treatment of its multiracial citizenry. The trust and coming together of minds to provide available resources, answers, creative solutions, and inclusive strategies, were lacking. Our efforts and mission to grow spiritually and accomplish faith-based tasks were weakened. We tried to promote our religious belief in one Creator. That was smart, but in separate societies? White Americans wanted to teach these Black people about ONE God? *Could they do that, really?* But somehow, in slavery times—when our Black worshipers were in the balcony (or "hush harbors" …their chosen places of worship), and our White worshipers were in the sanctuary of their churches, this was not an easy teach. This did not promote feelings of Christian love, oneness, and unity.

During this time, very few in our nation were focused on promoting unity of God's creation, African American people, in America. The focus was on dividing us as a nation in order to use more easily, or control, some of us for personal wealth and economic gain and prosperity. Unfortunately, for some greed-driven and highly possessive citizens, that attitude and purpose prevailed then and, quite possibly, drives many today.

RACISM, HATE, DISHARMONY AND DISCORD AMONGST FELLOW AMERICANS

Many of America's unscrupulous citizens welcomed racial conflict and unrest as a reason to promote their agenda of control and disunity. They thrived on disharmony within our nation. They used schemes, lies, concocted accusations, stereotyping, and other malicious methodology and teachings of hate to prolong the segregation and separation of races. The South, seemingly, more so than the North, embraced racial hatred and unfair treatment between the races. They did not want to elevate the status or minds of the slaves, nor the freedmen. They did not want to teach them to read or write or communicate with others. They wanted to keep Black people where they were…inferior, submissive, and unlearned. They wanted free labor for the fields and vast farmlands that enlarged their pool of wealth. They refused to see them as God's creation and did not want the slaves to see themselves in this way. Over time, feelings and beliefs of superiority and hatred, based on race and skin color, were passed down from generation to generation. Whites were superior, and Blacks were worthless and inferior. But these divisive antics would not serve as reality in the minds of many faith-based citizens. Our Black and many of our White ancestors did not embrace, promote nor endorse this philosophy. *I believe they wanted unity.* They valued racial harmony and the desire to live fairly and equally amongst each other and with each other.

Due to a lot of conflict, mythical beliefs and unfocused efforts on unity and togetherness, our country suffered many setbacks. The loss of time, resources, and lives, while fighting each other was not the progress needed by a new nation. It faced these losses because our country wasn't willing and ready to include everyone in building for themselves and for our new country. Little to none was evident or encouraged among the Black race. Race and skin color mattered! It has always been an issue, in some shape, form or faction, in America. Imagine America's progress if every person had been allowed to work toward America, as well as their own lives.

AMERICA THE GREAT MIGHT HAVE BECOME EVEN GREATER

America might have become an even greater nation during its last 250 years if unity, freedom, and the 'idea of America' had been implemented. Our location of America, truly beautiful and expansive, could possibly have been free of poverty, homelessness, drugs, crime, packed prison populations, and other similar national blight. If America had remained more focused as a faith-based nation on racial equity at her beginnings, and skipped the abusive, brutal, inhumane system of slavery, I believe this country might have become an even greater nation of peoples. She was not at her best while devaluing and denying her diverse human resources and equal opportunities for national and personal development and growth. Her practices of Jim Crow Laws and separation immediately after slavery did not help. Diversity, racism, hatred of fellow countrymen and citizens of color are never an asset.

Many Africans who were kidnapped and brought over in chains, were formerly skilled craftsmen. All were created by our one Creator. They were fully humans! The skills they were in need of acquiring to function better for this nation could have been taught. They were as capable of learning as anyone else.

I confess my ignorance. I learned in college that my people, my ancestors, were not savages running around in the jungle every day filming a Tarzan movie. I am so ashamed that I once thought that was true! No, when they were stolen away from the homeland on the continent of Africa, they were already skilled in several areas. Some of them possessed more skills and talents than their captors. Some of them were herbalists, doctors, teachers, architects, mathematicians, businessmen, fishermen, ship builders, and farmers. They were artists, cooks, weavers, entertainers, astronomers, and possessed other useful talents and skills. Had they not been kidnapped and enslaved, they could have contributed so much more in their lifetime. They could have put these skills to use to help build a bigger and stronger America! They were thought of only as workers of forced hard labor in this new country. The hard labor was needed, and greatly and undeniably contributed to America, but there was so much more. Slavery and hard field labor should not have been forced upon them as their only contribution and worth as human beings. It should not have been FREE and rewarding only for the good of the "master" and his descendants. The enslavers could have allowed them an opportunity to build their own lives as well as helping to build others around them. Efforts in the new world should have been unified, fair, equitable and more faith-based.

MORE DIVERSITY AND INCLUSIVENESS: WORTH AND VALUE

Indigenous people, already familiar with the land and its challenges, had successfully existed in North America for many years prior to the colonizers. They already knew how to achieve greatness in their crops of squash, corn, beans and mastery of production and reproduction of yearly fruits and vegetables. According to history, the Indigenous people had already used controlled burning, crop rotation, and other helpful feats. They were masters at herbal cures and medicinal properties needed for diseases and ailments. They were fishermen and skilled hunters of large and small game. They were bilingual and multilingual between the various tribes. White nor Black Americans were not as adept.

They could have been recruited to help neophytes, our White and Black ancestors, to adjust more thoroughly, and perhaps quicker, to a new environment. However, their worth and value were diminished due to their skin color. They were seen as being unqualified or unequal in the need of building and sharing in the plans and vision of moving America forward. On-the-job training was available in abundance. Skin color and racism narrowed the expectations, hopes, and dreams of unity and working together.

Our textbooks did not teach us to hate "Indian" people, or disrespect them, intentionally. It was done primarily unintentionally. The major source of media at that time--- comic books and on the black and white movie and television's black and white screens. Very early on in my life, I was carefully taught that the Indians were not highly valued as human beings. Growing up in our little, small town in East Texas, I never saw a real-life person I recognized as an "Indian." Their contributions to the great American society seen in our textbooks did not exist. It was not valued in our American history classes any more than pages dedicated to Black people or other Americans of color.

My first introduction to seeing real live Indian people was in a segregated movie theater in Jacksonville, Texas. My dear sweet father had taken me to the Realto "picture show," aka movie theater, to see a Western movie. We called it a "Cowboys and Indians" picture. The Cowboys were the good guys. The Indians were, you know the history, the bad guys. They talked in short sentences, grunted, and wore hardly any clothes. They usually wore a feather in their hair. They lost every battle they fought against the cowboys. We always rooted for the Cowboys. The "Cowboys, mind you, were always, White. The only "good Indian" I remember ever seeing as a child was "Tonto," the Lone Ranger's partner. Fortunately, later on, we did appreciate and admire the brief lessons on Chief Sitting Bull, Crazy Horse, and Chief Geronimo. All of these chiefs and their warriors were presented as wise and brave. Even though the lessons were brief, I always associated them as having families of kindness and Thanksgiving. As a little girl, I enjoyed the beautiful stories of Pocahontas. I am sure there were many other unsung Indigenous heroes and revolutionaries from across America, but back, then I was not privy to this information.

Unlike in most of the "Westerns," history tells us that the Indians' desire was to live peaceably, for the most part, in America. History also tells of the sufferings, trickery, and the peace-breaking treaties amongst our ancestors. The phrase of "White men speaketh with forked tongue" was said to have been coined by Indigenous people. It was a catch phrase used in most movies depicting untruthful deeds and misdeeds between Whites and Indigenous people.

I was never taught about the unusual mixing of colors and races, which suggested that they did not hate each other or all Blacks. Most did not mix, but it was an acceptable choice. It was not something that was forced upon them. The backgrounds and talents of American citizens like Edmonia Lewis, the great Indigenous sculptor, born in the 1840s, is an example. Learning about her and others in our history lessons would have given us a greater appreciation for these people as well. It would have promoted Indigenous people in a different and more positive manner. Her art was prominently displayed in the Smithsonian and in the Metropolitan Museum of Art. I call this information sharing "Humanizing" people of color. Share the best of who people are with others and preferably in their presence. It can build self-esteem for those who are on the receiving end as well. It goes a long way in teaching against hate for self and others.

Fortunately, certain insightful educators recognized the importance of imparting additional significant knowledge concerning indigenous peoples. Along the way we learned about these important lives and the contributions they made.

Mary Riddell, the native American aviator, was a skilled at flying planes almost a century ago. She insisted on wearing her buckskins and braids and proudly publicized herself as an Indian woman.

Susan La Flesche Picotte was born on a Nebraska's Omaha reservation in 1865. She was a young girl when she first saw a sick Indigenous community member suffer and die while waiting for a White doctor. By pursuing a Euro-American education while honoring the customs of her people, La Flesche Picotte battled backlash and became the first Indigenous person to earn a medical degree. She defied the odds again in 1913 when she opened the Omaha reservation's first hospital. La Flesche Picotte died in 1915, and she was commemorated on her deathbed for bridging the gap between her Indigenous roots and her Euro-American medical education.

I was not taught or privy to discussion of history lessons on Indigenous sheroes and heroes who resisted oppression and tried to knock down barriers and hatred between the races. This is an example of positive information to teach appreciation and it helps to validate another person's worth. It helps to teach against hate. It could very well have changed the course of history if these types of people could have played a bigger role in helping to build America. Instead, many were rejected and never got their opportunity due to their race and the color of their skin.

The same was true with our Mexican brothers and sisters. Historically, they have claimed their places as European-style white Immigrants as well as nonwhites. We just knew them as Mexicans who picked cotton in the fields with us or somewhere nearby. For me they were beautiful, tanned people who spoke another language that I wanted to learn as well. I knew nothing about their culture and equated them to Whites. I never saw signs that I should not have done so. In my geography classes in school, I learned they, too, occupied a great swath of the South and Southwestern land that was here at the inception of colonial days. *How much could America have gained in the inclusivity of the talents and skills of these people rather than exclusion due to skin color?*

Think of the vast amount of talent that went unused due to racist beliefs harbored in the minds of many of the early leaders…not the framers or abolitionists…they understood the need for unity, early on. But those early "leaders" who fought to continue to dehumanize, devalue, separate, segregate and abort unification efforts that would unite America. I believe their shortsightedness and hatefulness possibly hindered America's productivity. Their abuse of inclusiveness might have kept America from being all that she could have been. Had she used her human resources and equally distributed the wealth amongst the inhabitants who were there, America might never have had poverty amongst her people in the years that followed and even today.

Judith Zaffirini became the first woman Dean of the Texas Senate. I personally had the honor of meeting her. In her youth, Judith's work ethics were extraordinary. She was one of the most beautiful, fiery, hardworking, and determined young Hispanic Civil Rights activists in America. She was the first Mexican-American woman to serve in the state's upper legislative chamber when she was elected, and she is one of only 24 women who have ever served in the state Senate.

Henry Cisneros was another of my peers. After serving admirably, as a young dynamic mayor of one of the largest cities (San Antonio) in America, he was later named Housing Director by President Bill Clinton. Cisneros will go down in history as one of the leading Americans, of Hispanic descent, during the time America needed and wanted to experience positive relationships among its growing diverse population.

One of my favorite and unforgettable leaders of Mexican decent was Cesar Chavez. He was another contemporary. But several Mexican American leaders played a significant role in the fight for civil rights. We were not taught lessons in a way to place much value on these individuals. However, that is no excuse for not expanding our knowledge base in this internet savvy world now. Here are some of the most notable Mexican Americans you can look forward to reading about from the past:

1. **Jose Antonio Navarro**: He was a prominent figure in the Texas Revolution and was one of the signers of the Texas Declaration of Independence.

2. **Juan Seguin**: He was another important figure in the Texas Revolution and served as mayor of San Antonio.

3. **Cesar Chavez**: He was a Mexican American labor leader and Civil Rights Activist who dedicated his life's work to improving the working and living conditions of farm workers in the United States. He co-founded the United Farm Workers (UFW) and led several strikes and boycotts to improve the wages and working conditions of farm workers.

4. **Luisa Moreno**: She was a Guatemalan-born Mexican American Civil Rights Activist who fought for the rights of workers, immigrants, and women. She was a key figure in the labor movement and helped to organize several strikes and protests.

These are just a few of the many Mexican American leaders who fought for civil rights.

Historian Julie M Wiese stated that Mexican immigrants forced Jim Crow systems to bend stretch and adapt definitions of race that looked beyond "blood" and ancestry… to include culture, class, and politics. In the 1920s, Mexican immigrants questioned the United States as to who was white and who was not. They sought clarity as to what side of the 'color line' they were on as far as Jim Crow laws were concerned. In the pursuit, of legal work on this concerns, Mexican immigrants won and earned the title of "obtaining and retaining White status" when needed on applications, drivers' licenses, etc., in spite of the darkest skin color or social status of the applicant. This was through politics and help from the Mexican Consulate located in New Orleans. This helped these citizens to navigate the racist system and to avoid the Jim Crow hassles as well.

BLACK AND WHITE: "THORN IN THE SIDE"

Racism has always been a "thorn in the side" for America. Think of the number of Whites who lost their lives, proving or disapproving, their stance on racial issues in America. (In most of the research I have done, race became a problem in the early 1600s. It has been a constant issue even today, as we stare our Sesquicentennial, 2026, in the face. History tells us that during the Civil War, over 45,000-50,000 (mostly White) lives were lost and because family members were fighting on both sides, one for the North and another family member for the South, this was more than a harrowing war. Many of these Civil War warriors were young, poor, and inexperienced, but were convinced "they should take up arms" to win their argument…whatever that was... America wasted valuable talent in this White American group, as well, because a number of these were formally schooled, trained, and resourceful, and were continuing to help build this new country.

Their families and businesses were left at home while they fought each other in the Civil War. Sometimes, we were told that a funeral for a family on one weekend could be followed on the next weekend by the ceremony of another family member. This family member, however, was supporting or opposing different viewpoints of how America should move forward… Due to their different stances taken, fathers, brothers, uncles, and cousins fought each other. Unity and togetherness had been replaced by divisiveness and differences of opinion about many issues. One of their foremost interests had to do with slavery.

America was not at her best with making this decision. This time, effort, attention, and these precious lives were caused by human sacrifices made early on in America. It was focused, unfortunately, on issues involving race, skin color and dealing with divisiveness. What if we had used these lives to build America's vision for a new strong and different united country beginning in the 1600s. I believe America would have been even more awesome as a world leader while celebrating our Semiquincentennial.

BORN TO BE A SLAVE DUE TO RACE OR SKIN COLOR? NO THANKS!

Other than offering free labor on their huge plantations, most of the early African Americans and their off-springs were thought of as worthless. Then, worldwide foreign leaders, like Hitler and other American white supremacist groups, were cohesive and supportive in their efforts to dehumanize the Black race.

These renown leaders, hailed by many popular ones during this time in American history, verbalized and publicized their beliefs that

Black people were worthless creatures: "Negroes were no more than chattel, less than 3/5 in worth at the ballot box, and not capable of competing with whites on any level!". These were leaders who were schooled by racist foolish ideas that inferiority was defined and acquired through skin color. They had made these assumptions on "how 'they' looked" to them. "They were Black, kinky-haired and did not speak European languages (some of the kidnapped and enslaved spoke multiple languages) or English, well." *This meant you were less than human?* They had no other distinguishable measurable tools other than these visual and audible observations, as acceptable in their minds, to justify their intentions of the continuation of enslavement.

Think of the talents and skills of the Jesse Owenses (during Hitler's reign), Jackie Robinsons, Marian Andersons, Mary McCloud Bethune Cookmens, Richard Allens, and so many others who disproved their thoughts. They were a few of the African American names of citizens who had finally been given an opportunity to showcase their talents and skills. There were more! But these were now included in spaces previously denied to them, due to their skin color and racist thinkers.

Imagine the surprised feelings and the look on the faces of Hitler and his followers when Jesse Owens came away from the German Olympics with four gold medals for the United States of America! He is said to have single-handedly diffused the myth that Black Americans were not competitors!

Their performances were of natural inheritance endowed by their Creator, who also chose to add more melanin in their skin. He created us and He is entitled to do such! These Black people were not trained in big universities or facilities as most of their competitors had been, they were just natural, DNA-blessed skills. They were just born to "be like that!"

Think of the aptness of Harriet Tubman who outsmarted men on horseback, dogs, and environmental conditions to complete tasks required to run the Underground Railroad. Again, remember, they were not schooled, or university trained nor technologically enhanced. They were not born to be someone's slave because of the color of their skin. So why would "man" assume this institution of dehumanization was okay for our race of men, women, and children? Was it because of sin, greed, and immorality? A better question might be, "what type of mind would allow himself to want to own another human being?"

What kind of mind would need to brutally abuse and misuse a woman, man, or child in such a dehumanizing way as some of our ancestors were exposed to? Depraved? Moronic? Evil? Abraham Lincoln, one of our founding fathers who owned slaves, but always spoke out against it, once said: "I would not want to be a slave, but neither would I want to be a slave owner."

I believe that none of God's human beings created in His image, were people meant to be seen as inferior to others, due to skin color. They possessed natural talents and skills, just like other human beings who were given equal opportunities to perform. I proclaim that we know that our Black ancestors were born with these capabilities, because they were not allowed to be learned scholars or trained craftsmen in America. Yet, they have been known to outperform many of their competitors. I imagine this came as a big disappointment for those who wanted to believe that God created an inferior race defined by their skin color. ...and that this inferior race was created by God to serve these other people due to their skin color! It should have been a surprise for those who believed He created a superior race, based on skin color, as well. The "inferiors" were to serve the "superiors," based on their skin color and race.

But this was not at a time when America was at her best. America had not quite decided to seriously consider unity while building this nation for her people. Whenever we, as a nation, have worked in opposition, divisive, lawless, and with immoral manners, these United States of America have suffered. Our people suffered. In the eyes of the world, we presented ourselves as weak. Our ancestors and fellow true Americans are disappointed to witness this type of behavior in the homeland. America is bigger and better than that.

Once upon a time, during slavery and Jim Crow, we tried this overt racist type of behavior on our citizens. Segregation and separatism were to be carried out based solely on skin color. It was not a good fit for a freedom-loving country like America. It was shameful and a blight in our history. Two hundred years have passed, and we don't want to think or talk about it. Why? Because, yes, it was that ugly. But we must remember, in order that we will not allow our country to repeat itself. This was not one of America's best times in history.

BY LEARNING ABOUT OUR PAST, WE CAN HAVE A BRIGHTER FUTURE.

Name something you learned in this chapter to help you not to hate other Americans, regardless of their color.

____

____

____

____

____

CHAPTER 7

Major Race Issues:
Checked, Unchecked, and Inconsequential

If a person wants to burden their lives with the weight of racism on their shoulders, their lives in our diverse society will be so unfulfilled. America is becoming more multiracial and multicultural every day. Can we make this democracy work while being segregated? Could it produce more if American citizens worked together, harmoniously? We think the latter. It isn't hard. And if it does not, we don't want it to be something as minute as skin color that will take us out. America has come through too much and has made too many human sacrifices to walk away or give in without a real fight. Right now, our biggest threat to the destruction of the American democracy is the divisiveness and polarization within. We all must work against hate and divisiveness in our diverse society. More unity and togetherness must be our goal to celebrate 2026.

In preparation of the celebrations of the Semiquincentennial, our Black and White ancestors would want us to understand this urgent need to promote unity and togetherness as a major goal. Our democracy's diverse population cannot exist in a hate filled lawless environment. The major issues and threats to our nation are the feelings of unequal treatment due to race and skin color. Every causal factor, no matter if true, false, or somewhere in between, is seen somehow to be tied into the belief that America is unfair toward different races. Whether true, not true, or indifferent, this causes, of course, conflict. Unchecked and or inconsequential conflict in a diverse proximity breeds hate. So, issues surrounding America's greatest problems and challenges come from within.

The topic of racism or hate has been present, in some shape, form or fashion, since the early 1600s. Most often, it involved Black and White relations and similar issues. Slavery, Civil War, Jim Crow, and unfair and unequal treatment of United States citizens of color have continuously cast major shadows of aspersion over our ancestors and our country. There are many things in America's young immature past that are so ugly and shameful, we want to pretend they never happened. But these historical events occurred, and we cannot change or conceal them. For some Americans, that is no problem. Some think it is too painful. For others, it is too provocative and incendiary. They choose to "hide their heads in the sand."

But for myself and many more like me, we feel that if we can remember how our families and friends were impacted as American citizens; knowing our history helps to keep us more grounded. We are more alert about ways to avoid dreadful and negative recurrences. (It kept us from voting for Governor George Wallace when he ran for President). As a result, we should try to be mindful of what's happening around us… in the past, as well as now. We cannot allow our young, adults, and children, to forego present warnings. America is not yet all it can be for them. They must continue to be encouraged to fight for their rights and to be ardent supporters of our country.

We believe schools should open with prayer, pledges to the flag, a biblical quote, and a motivational message of patriotic and emotional support. Every day! Remember, we speak from experience! We lived the research! We can compare! We have lived long enough and witnessed our schools of today and those of yesterday. Just imagine in your mind what we proposed, from almost a hundred years ago, admittedly, and today's classrooms. We do not need to ask the question about which environment was/is more conducive to learning/teaching, do we? Now quit snickering and spend some more quality time with the matriarch and patriarch in your family for some other good practical advice!

AVOIDING CRIME AND POVERTY IN AMERICA MIGHT JUST BE A CHOICE

Getting involved in local, state, and federal levels of politics as soon as they can vote is another powerful weapon in fighting against hate. Our young Americans must assume responsibilities that will lead them away from tolerating and accepting poverty as "my place in life." If other races can live above poverty using America's vast resources, so can our race. They must be taught that they may never be rich, but they do not have to live in poverty. Poverty can be caused by racism, but poverty can also be caused by a lack of motivation and laziness. Today, physically healthy, law abiding, faith-based, and mentally-well citizens can discover a way out of poverty. They must not live in fear of being poor and poverty-stricken for the rest of their lives. They do not have to hate or blame anyone but themselves if they choose to do so. They must put forth every effort to avoid criminals, criminal minds, and criminal activity, even with friends and sometimes with family. They should fear and flee traps, snares, and pipelines of choices, which they, sometimes foolishly make, aimed at robbing themselves of their futures.

The consequences of their choices are not dealt with equally. So even when they know others who have committed the 'same or similar' acts, the consequences may or may not be the same. Avoid acts and activity recognized as leading causes to the feeding of the jails and prisons. Youth must be taught that this system is a form of the modern-day institution of slavery in our society. Statistical evidence shows that our young Black, Brown, and a few poor White Americans will continue to enter our prison system, thus generating many salaries and large sums of money for those who are in control of the penal system.

Unlike our ancestors who were kidnapped, stolen, or sold into their fate, most of our 'smart' young people who chose to avoid a life of crime can rise above this despicable system. Unfortunately, most of these facilities breed more hate and crime. They are not designed for rehabilitation of mind, soul, or progress. Our youth must be encouraged and motivated to rise above the inhumane and atrocious practices of entrapment of for-profit public and private penal systems built with our people in mind. They do not teach against hate and division. The overwhelming majority of these institutions promote racism and divisiveness, whether intentionally or unintentionally.

TRACES OF OVERT AND COVERT RACISM LINGERING IN AMERICA'S HISTORY BREEDS DIVISION

We must never forget the horrors of slavery and segregation as institutions of hatred and divisiveness in America. It is one of the most despicable and sin ladened acts committed on the soil we have labeled as the United States of America. All American citizens must know the truth about slavery. No one has to embellish or put lipstick on it. Just tell the truth and it will speak for itself. During slavery times, there were families separated and sold on auction blocks, breeding of slaves for profits, whippings, lynchings, sexual abuses, and other scornful and immoral sinful acts. Mostly all of this dreadful system and these actions were committed by greedy, but powerful, White men who chose to be slave owners. Many White

Americans amassed great wealth that passed down through many generations, using the free labor of our ancestors. Our youth must know, also, that there were White Americans who did not approve of this brutal system and fought against it, as well. Many lost their lives trying to appeal to their fellow Americans for the abandonment of this heinous system.

After the Emancipation, Reconstruction Era, and other attempts to make the American dream presentable for all citizens, our nation continued desecrating blows inflicted upon our Black ancestors, inspired by hate. These acts were overt and blatant. Law enforcement and punishment for these crimes were nonexistent. Some Black Americans were trying to forgive meanspirited atrocities directed at them and move on. Our ancestors began to build their own neighborhoods, grocery stores, schools, churches, and other necessities. Most of these were burned and bombed after experiencing a brief success. These criminal acts were led by hate filled mobs and terroristic groups of unsavory fellow White Americans.

Down through the years, history will be shown, and stories will be told, about the massive destruction of many Black-owned businesses and lives, mostly in Southern states, which were destroyed. Their churches were bombed, their schools were ruined and destroyed. Other dark tales inflicted by police brutality, the KKK and white supremacists' groups ran unchecked in America for many years. No law enforcement at local, state, and national levels were available to protect those victimized by this type of barbaric behavior. Very, very few White Americans were ever held accountable or suffered any consequences for their misdeeds.

Our Black and White forefathers could easily have become broken in spirit, but they did not give up. Some of our ancestors kept trying to find a special place for themselves and their voices of freedom and hope in America. Many of their White brethren were there to support them during this time. Together, they tried to make a difference. In unity, they continued to fight and make small strides against hate and racist behaviors. We must teach our youth these lessons of strength found in nonviolent protests, honor of hope, the will to keep trying to move forward and never giving up, as well. Our history of implementing attempts of 'oneness' does not need to be shameful. Ours was unique and different. Our ancestors were Chosen Vessels!

Their faith and hope in America, inexplicably, kept them moving forward. as the vast destruction of Black-owned property - farms, homes, and personal gains - were obliterated with little or no consequences. These acts were mean and despicable forms of hatred and racism after slavery. We have a history of receiving violent acts directed toward us as a race in America. The sin of overt racist practices directed at Black people might have started with slavery, but it did not end there. Our history of implementing attempts of 'oneness' has a record of shame and pain attached to it. However, it is our history, and we must not allow it to escape from other memories of our past. We must define its relevancy and reverence.

The Tulsa Massacre, or Black Wall Street in Tulsa, Oklahoma was bombed from the air by an angry group fueled by hatred of their fellow Americans. In 1921, a white mob dropped a bomb on the city's once thriving Greenwood Black community. Over 300 American citizens were killed. Over 191 businesses were destroyed. Over 10,000 Black Tulsans were displaced. PBS and KERA sponsored a segment in 2021 giving two main reasons cited by authority figures as to why this horrific event happened. Hatred and racism led to this violent event starting with "yellow journalism" or exaggerated and sensationalized false accounts of an incident with a young Black male and a young white female. Remember "You must be carefully taught to hate." ... . This huge white mob was *deputized* by the police. Could they have been deputized to protect the innocent Black and White American citizens that were in harm's way? *We don't think so.*

Another bombing of Black American citizens, from the air, was on May 13, 1985. The world watched as police dropped an explosive device on the roof of a housing unit in West Philadelphia. A day long confrontation with the Black radical group, MOVE, had not obeyed orders to exit the premises of the building they were occupying. I remember that many Blacks (and probably many Whites as well) were hoping they would come out because there were children involved, as well. But for some reason they did not. The news reported that police officers fired over 10,000 rounds of ammunition into the building before dropping a bomb from a helicopter onto the building's roof, igniting a destructive inferno for blocks. Top city officials, including a Black mayor, were cleared of criminal liability for death and destruction resulting from the operation, also.

There was another hate filled post slavery significant event that took place on American soil in Wilmington, North Carolina.

In 1898, the **Wilmington Massacre took place.** This was a violent act carried out by white supremacists. On Thursday, November 10, 1898, the insurrection was a violent overthrow of a duly elected government by a group of white supremacists. They expelled the opposition. Black and white political leaders from the city, destroyed the property and businesses of Black citizens built up since the American Civil War. They destroyed the only Black newspaper in the city. They killed an estimated 60 to more than 300 people. *According to a BBC News article, no one was held accountable for the insurrection.*

SHARING LIVED EXPERIENCES CAN HELP PREPARE FOR A BETTER FUTURE

Sometimes it is better to not have to read, think, or discuss the horrors of our painful past. However, since we have a "past," we must accept its facts, confront its truths, and work toward a solution. We must learn from it. As soon as possible, we must work together in dispelling its sting and possible reoccurrences in todays' society. Every effort should be made to stamp out racism and hatred in our society, regardless of where it is located. Racist behavior, no matter who or where it originates, must not be seen as an acceptable part of these United States of America. If left unchecked, eventually it will destroy our diverse country and the freedom loving democracy we embrace. This should be an item on every American citizen's agenda who loves our nation. If this is not of value or importance to our diverse population, our own moral standards, our hopes, and future plans toward providing equal rights to an unfinished Emancipation Project, nothing is.

For directions to our young and upcoming future generations, our nation must know the lived experiences we want to avoid most. America must know the past in order that we never see or contribute to its "ugly parts" again… now or amongst future generations! There is nothing to dictate that we cannot meet these, admittingly, great charges and challenges. Help and a guide is outlined in our constitution, as well as in other significant documents. Our founders laid out a clear, concise, faith-based, unifying path to the governing of our nation formed of many people. What America must do is enforce her own laws, as one nation, to a diverse population. Become a "promise keeper," America! Hopefully, knowing certain key incidents and warning signs from our past will prepare us for a brighter future.

Our Constitutional laws will help us to become better prepared to fight off innocence, ignorance, and many temptations to stray from serving a multiracial and diverse population. America can and must avoid acts of aggression, discomfort, disapproval, and dismay amongst her variety of multicultural citizens. Feelings of being left out, overlooked, ignored, used, and/or unappreciated are some major causes of unrest in diverse populations. In many instances, this leads to dissatisfaction, disappointments, demonstrations, insurrections, protests, sit-ins, and similar responses, including violence, amongst our nation's people. It leads to feelings of helplessness and to hate. *Again, great efforts, not enforced. Few held accountable. This leads to divisiveness.*

Stronger support at the voters' boxes is another meaningful and effective tool of choice for the fight in this struggle. Self-driven careful research of the selection of political candidates can suppress social disharmony. Avoid candidates who spew harsh criticism and racist language in an effort to discredit their competition. They should not lead America's citizens. These political candidates, who are surrounded by an environment of chaos and hate, cannot help their constituents to do much better. Their own chaos, violence, hatred, and inhumane deeds that cause division in America must be avoided at all costs. Find positive candidates who campaign on the good they intend to do for you as an American. Look for candidates who will promise the enforcement of laws and their goodwill, shared equally amongst its citizens. Hopefully, they will keep their promises. This can certainly eliminate violent and deadly insurrections against our democracy and other signs of immoral misdeeds against humanity.

When I look back over our nation's history, I cannot believe our country, built on a faith-based foundation, could have committed so many atrocities and evil deeds against humanity. Some citizens are not bothered by past (or present) misdeeds against their fellow men. They only visualize how wretched these acts are when it happens to them, or maybe to a family member. I, however, am highly offended at this type of unpatriotic behavior. Granted, some actions are worse than others, but they always bring pain and sorrow upon the victims of discrimination. I oppose any "pain and sorrow inflicted on another human being due to "skin color and race." The bullies who commit these offenses must not get away with thinking their racist actions are "fun," funny, or are playful "jokes" … and harmless. Racists remarks, language, and other actions, that belittle, shame, or make mockery of another human being, outside or inside your own race, should always be questionable. If the attack can be attributed to situations beyond any person's control, such teasing, taunting, demeaning ranting, and ravings, are immoral. There should never be a time to tolerate and accept this type of action.

I also believe those who amuse and entertain themselves by witnessing and observing these immature, mean-spirited acts, should be avoided. They just stand by and watch others apply, infringe, or inject their evil sick forces on a weaker being. While they may not commit the actual act, tolerance may be seen by the victim and the aggressor as being acceptable. Neither moves our nation forward in unity. It teaches hate and malice between American citizens. According to Dr. Opal Lee, **"One person cannot be free until we are all free!"**

This type of behavior does nothing toward uniting our America. I wonder, sometimes in awe, how people could become so mean in spirit toward one another! Does skin color really matter that much? Is there a deeper problem with God's choices and displays chosen in His human creations? What causes so much angst among His creatures He has placed here on His earth? Again, the shameful acts are in our past and as a freedom-loving citizen, I aim to continue to work to enforce our laws equally. Everyone will be held accountable, so that there will be less animosity toward others. In this way, racism, hatred, and bigotry, will stay in the past. Our founding fathers' visions expressed in our Constitution, patriotism, and prayers will not allow a return or rerun of such actions.

WORKING TO UNITE THESE UNITED STATES

In our Semiquincentennial year of 2026, we must all be prepared to celebrate America's greatness. Our Black and White ancestors would have wanted us to do so. The United States of America is never going to be perfect, but we keep seeking higher ground spiritually, morally, socially, and intellectually. With these intentional actions, we will find solutions to many of our racial problems. Racism and hatred are sins that blur and prevent progress toward unity. Our collective voices must be heard. We must all work together, Black and White Americans toward unification in a society as diverse as our America. There is no denying, even though there are other marginalized groups seeking to find their places, the greatest and most obvious lines of demarcation have been drawn between Black and White races. If America can get this part straight, and she has been working to do so, Americans will celebrate the Semiquincentennial without embarrassment. Then there will be much in our legacy and heritage to celebrate and commemorate, as well.

Our nation stands as a beacon, a proud representative and reminder of the respect for freedom in the world. I get goosebumps visualizing our Statue of Liberty protruding from the shores in New York Harbor. Because of the many sacrifices all of our Founding Fathers and ancestors have made from its inception down through slavery, Jim Crow, the Civil Rights Movement, and present-day struggles, we have continued to 'rise and build.' In spite, of adversities, mistakes, setbacks, "sin and shame," the United States of America can lead a diverse society forward. She can be successful because her citizens will be successful, but America must repent and represent all of her people. As faith-based and grateful citizens, lovers of humanity, and our country, we must open our hearts and minds to allow our diversity to be a blessing.

Name something you learned in this chapter to help you not to hate other Americans, regardless of their color.

____

____

____

____

____

____

____

____

____

____

____

____

____

CHAPTER 8

Our Labor, Someone Else's Wealth

In our Semiquincentennial year of 2026, we can all be prepared to celebrate America's greatness by learning a little more about our forefathers' efforts to work toward peace and harmony between the races. I believe our Black and White ancestors wanted us to do so. The Constitution and Bill of Rights were constructed with moving America forward in unity and as one, in mind. As a country, the United States planned to move ahead united, E Pluribus Unum. No written laws of this magnitude, 250 years ago, would have been written differently. It was never intended to cause separation, hatred, and divisiveness among America's people, she was trying to grow. I believe it would have been counterproductive to the intent of building a new stronger nation. The constitution is not a perfect document; however, it is ours. It is unique, inclusive, and when these promises are kept and enforced equally amongst its citizens, we have cause for pride in that celebration!

During slavery times in America, many Whites refused to own slaves because they deemed it a sin. Even though it was profitable to many (and for generations of family members that followed), some people thought it was such a repugnant act, it should not be used in a faith-based society. This new world was destined and determined to be unique. Down through the years, our history supports the fact that once the 1619 project was introduced, America's greatest divisions and disagreements in building this new nation and structuring an acceptable governing system appeared. The contention centered around issues concerning race and wealth. Americans were split, even within families, on their stances and opinions regarding the "moral question of human bondage and man's inhumanity to man." In other words, would we allow our country to engage in such an inhumane disgusting system as slavery?!?!.

I, as a Christian Believer agree that if sins could be measured, perhaps, slavery, and the racist behaviors, actions and reactions attached to such an institution were included, it would be one of the worst. From its sadistic, inhumane, ungodly actions and practices the repercussions and fallout, even today (feelings of inferiority and superiority), slavery and the '1619 Project" has been phenomenal, to say the least. The fallout from this one act weaves its way through American history in many guises. It has cost America many lives in the Civil War, countless Black lives of terroristic lynchings, massacres, and murders. It has been seen as an unending cause of civil and social debates. It has caused constant disharmony and disruptions to the faith-based American's peace of mind. It must never be repeated on American soil.

History will show that, from time to time, slavery was practiced in other parts of the world. A handful of freed Black people in America owned slaves and fought against the abolition of slavery. It certainly happened, but it did not make it right for this nation. America set out to be a different country. Its aim, on paper and in the minds of our founders and forefathers, was to be a freedom-loving country protecting the rights of her citizens early in America's history. However, history shows most of our African American ancestors experienced the horrors of this despicable system of slavery on these shores of the United States of America, involuntarily.

Our introduction to America is so unique and unlike any other race with as much impact, now, in America. Most of our ancestors were kidnapped or stolen and brought over on slave ships. History tells us, too, that there were many Black people who were already on these, soon to become known as, American shores. During the 1600s, our ancestors were captured and/or "tricked" into America by ruthless and cruel White men, motivated, primarily, by their plan for wealth. Our fore parents (men, women, and children) were needed and used in the "New World" to work and build, and help make America into a different type, but great and powerful, country. There was plenty of work to be done in developing the country…and that we did!

I like to work…We know our ancestors probably did not mind working either, but as captives? for FREE? Yes, the FREE labor of our ancestors helped to build America. For over two centuries, we built and rebuilt railroads, infrastructure, highways, streets, roads, bridges, factories, churches, universities, schools, and other major necessities needed to construct a strong powerful foundation on which America could develop and prosper. American Black people were responsible for cooking, laundering, babysitting, nursing of sick babies, and tending the elderly. Our men, women, and children worked the land, tilled the soil, gathered the harvests from sunup 'til sundown while they were enslaved in America. That was not an eight-hour shift and yet it was not uncommon for some persons to see us as "lazy and shiftless."

Remember, during this period of the 1600s-1800s, America was a young country with little wealth from its young citizenry. But our ancestors used their skills and talents to enlarge our nation's assets for generations to come. Enslaved people helped immensely in turning this country into a wealthy freedom-loving democracy with a land of many resources and opportunities. Many of these opportunities were not extended to Black Americans, however. Even though our ancestors did the work needed, we did not receive a monetary return. What was extended did not give us equal returns on our investments. On the other hand, history reveals that for many White plantation owners, manufacturers, business owners and others, economically, America was great! It was the lucrative commodities such as tobacco, cotton, rice, sugar cane, and other goods that propelled its growth and brought great wealth to this country. Even though, later on in American history, there were many reports of lots of "gold in them thar' hills" out west, the South amassed generational unprecedented fortunes in this area alone.

Historical data shows that by 1860, the per capita wealth of many Southern Whites was twice that of Northerners or other sections of the country. Three-fifths of the wealthiest individuals in the country were Southerners. The labor force (our enslaved men, women, and children) in the South was producing 75 percent of the world's hottest commodity, cotton, during that time. It is known by many that this economic trend created more millionaires per capita in the Mississippi River valley than anywhere in the nation. Our ancestors, men, women, and their offsprings, as enslaved workers provided American Southerners with their most significant investment—and the bulk of their wealth.

Beginning in the mid-1600s, to the latter 1700s, there were nearly 700,000 Black enslaved people living in the United States. This provided a humongous economic boost for our whole country, especially if you were on the receiving end of the boost! More cotton from the South meant more businesses, jobs, and trade elsewhere in America. There was a "domino effect" in place, driven by this product in demand all over the world at that time. This meant more employment opportunities, manufacturing of goods and services, transporting of products, shipping, and handling, etc. Needless to say, slavery was extremely popular and profitable to White people and a miniscule group of Americans of color. Its wealth lasted for generations that followed. Evidence is present today.

Many of our Black and White American ancestors knew, in spite of its profitability, it was wrong to enslave another human being for such personal gain. But America's slave labor force drove impressive profits in the United States of America. Our ancestors were forced, under dire circumstances, to sacrifice and invest their lives in America "for FREE!" Putting an end to this horrible institution brought both relief and joy, followed by grief and pain. Unfortunately, observing this practice and unequal distribution of wealth taught divisiveness and hate.

Name something you learned in this chapter to help you not to hate other Americans, regardless of their color.

____

____

____

____

____

____

____

____

____

____

CHAPTER 9

United We Stand, Divided We 'Hurt and Hate'

I believe that the framers of the United States Constitution were wise and blessed during the time they spent in composing this document. Their intent in writing was to create a functional and practical tool to unite and guide our nation. They sought to provide fundamental principles and precedents for governing fairly and equitably. In it, they outlined the structure of the government, the rights and duties of citizens, and the relationship between the government and its citizens. It appears to be one that could provide support and direction to build a solid foundation for a strong and diverse nation. It is labeled, rightly so, as the most important governing document in the United States of America.

We interpret it as a federal protection of our individual rights and liberties, regardless of our race and skin color. We, especially, as Black Americans, just want the "overseers" who are voted into offices, and law enforcement in various and sundry places, Black and White, to enforce these "laws of the land," equitably. We all need to love America, and what our constitution stands for, enough to follow through on these promises to all. Without these guidelines, amendments, and rules, we become divided. This can lead to emotional pain so intense; it can breed hatred amongst the people.

For over 250 years, we have longed for the promises of true emancipation to be enforced in our diverse communities. The lack of fulfilling these promises continues to fuel divisiveness in these United States of America. Wise and sagacious men wrote the "laws of the land," but they did not follow through to institute them. Over the centuries, we, Black and White Americans, have continued our "stride toward freedom."

Now, leading up to our 2026 Semiquincentennial, year's celebration, many problems that existed back then remain today. We still need wise and blessed men (and women!) to enforce our most powerful governing documents, including our United States Constitution. The challenges still appear to be applying and enforcing these governing laws, equally and equitably, across the land. Each of the founding framers and writers knew then that the population of America would likely continue as it appeared at the time of the writing. I believe that they could not have been that short-sighted or selfish as to have believed the constitution should only protect White men! (That is our belief and others are privy to theirs as well). Surely, people as wise as the framers of the Constitution would not have ignored such a versatile and diverse population, would they? We don't think so. We think the writers wanted to include every citizen, no matter what race was present and those that came later, as Americans. If they were citizens, they were included. It was for us who are recognized as citizens and accept the responsibility of citizenship in this great country.

The Constitution is not perfect and was written by imperfect men. I believe, however, that it is primarily built on faith-based values and principles. It is unique, inclusive, and it is ours. If you are an

American citizen, these are promises and expectations on which we, as faith-based Believers and law-abiding citizens, can and should depend. Other important amendments and special documents and laws have been added along the way, in an effort to unify this country. These documents have played a significant role in the shaping of our American democracy and governance. They have helped to protect individual rights and liberties, promote freedom and democracy, and ensure that all Americans are treated equally under the law. When these promises are kept and laws and rights are enforced equally amongst its diverse body of citizens, we have cause for celebration!

SPECIAL DOCUMENTS NEEDED TO UNITE THE STATES OF AMERICA'S DIVERSE PEOPLES

According to our research, and what we were led to believe down through the years, these are the most important and meaningful documents written to date. They impact our lives and well- being for people of this diverse nation. Their impact is even more crucial in America, as African Americans and descendants of the ruthless institutions of slavery, Jim Crow laws, and Civil Rights in efforts to establish a place of citizenship for us and for the generations to follow. They help to lead groups of citizens who are resistant away from unfair comfort zones that promote divisiveness and exclusion. Vestiges of negative attitudes and feelings of inferiority and superiority are still present after many centuries. These guidelines have helped us to avoid lingering, festering, and subliminal forms of overt and covert hate and racism due to skin color. Doors of opportunities were opened that would not have been opened to us, were it not for these efforts to correct past wrongs. Listed below are a few indications that America has attempted to position herself and her diverse population for success. Please note the togetherness and unity of the races, Black and Whites working toward a common goal. *The amendments were sometimes referred to as the Reconstruction Amendments.*

1. **The Declaration of Independence** is the document that was adopted by the Continental Congress on July 4, 1776. It declared the thirteen American colonies independent from Great Britain. It also declared that all men are created equally and have a right to life, liberty, and the pursuit of happiness. The language does not address Black people or women. It is considered to be one of the most important documents in American history. Special time, energy, and efforts are set aside to honor this special holiday to celebrate the freedom of the country from British rule. This document was necessary for the country to operate independently of British rule. History shows that African Americans - Crispus Attucks, Oliver Cromwell, Prince Hall, and many other Blacks - worked on both sides in seeking their freedom.

2. **The United States Constitution** is the most important governing document in the United States. Its governance began on March 4,1789. It outlines the framework of the federal government and protects individual rights and liberties. It has been instrumental in shaping American democracy and governance. It is another important document in our US history. Its importance to African Americans at the time is questionable. There were pros and cons as to how helpful it was to those who were enslaved when it was written. However, after many years of struggle, political activism, and patience, these laws established full citizenship and equal rights under the Constitution.

3. **The Emancipation Proclamation** is a document that was issued by President Abraham Lincoln on January 1, 1863. It declared that all slaves in the Southern held territory, or confederate states, were to be set free if they joined the Union. It did not immediately free all slaves in the United States, because it only applied to the eleven Confederate states then at war against the Union. It was, however, a significant step towards ending slavery in all of the states of America.

4. **The 13th Amendment to the U.S. Constitution abolished slavery in the United States.** It was passed on January 31, 1865. It stated that: "Neither slavery nor involuntary servitude, except as a punishment for crime whereof the party shall have been duly convicted, shall exist within the United States, or any place subject to their jurisdiction."

5. **The 14th Amendment to the U. S. Constitution was passed in 1865.** It granted full citizenship to those who were formerly enslaved. It granted full protection under the law.

6. **The 15th Amendment to the Constitution was passed in 1869.** It granted Black men the right to vote. Unfortunately, it did not extend this right to Black women. That would come afterwards through other efforts and means. (Why are there so many accusations of "an angry Black woman"?)

7. **Executive Order 9981**: On July 26, 1948, President Harry Truman ordered the desegregation of the U.S. armed forces. It abolished racial segregation in the United States Armed Forces and established the President's Committee on Equality of Treatment and Opportunity in the Armed Services[1]. The order stated that "there shall be equality of

treatment and opportunity for all persons in the armed forces without regard to race, color, religion, or national origin". It was a significant milestone in the Civil Rights Movement and paved the way for further desegregation in the United States.

8. **The Civil Rights Act of 1964** is an act that was signed into law by President Lyndon B. Johnson on July 2, 1964. It prohibited discrimination on the basis of race, color, religion, sex, or national origin. It became a turning point for education, employment, and public accommodations. Black and White Americans united, together, and fought for the passage of this act. Blacks and Whites, together, sacrificed their friends and, unfortunately, their lives to help make this act a right and expectation for citizens of all races. The Act helped to work toward ending racial segregation, discrimination, hate and divisiveness in America. It was a federal effort to encourage freedom and equal human rights for those citizens living in a diverse society. It did not promote hate and divisiveness between American citizens, but many ignored it. It was another law that was not fulfilled by all "law abiding citizens."

9. **The Voting Rights Act of 1965.** is an act that was signed into law by President Lyndon B. Johnson on August 5, 1965. It aimed to overcome legal barriers, at the state and local levels, which prevented African Americans from exercising their right to vote. The 15th Amendment to the United States Constitution guaranteed this right, but just as other attempts at correcting America's civil mistakes were aborted, for some, so had the rights to vote become questionable. It is considered to be one of the most important pieces of Civil Rights legislation in American history.

10. **The Fair Housing Act of 1968**: This law prohibited discrimination in the sale, rental, and financing of housing, based on race, religion, national origin, or sex. Again, this law was very meaningful in making our country great for all of its people. Unfortunately, there were plenty of neighborhoods that even when Black people had the finances, rich character, good reputable jobs, and met all of the other qualifications, they were not allowed to purchase homes or housing in certain areas. The discrimination that this Act was designed to eliminate was not enforced for all of its citizens then or now as we move toward the Semiquincentennial. Unfortunately, America's attempts to serve her diverse population fails to trickle down to the racist practices of many. These practices breed hate amongst diverse populations when promises are offered, and no one is held responsible or accountable.

11. **The Civil Rights Act of 1991**: This law strengthened existing Civil Rights laws by providing for damages in cases of intentional employment discrimination and by expanding protections for employees who allege discrimination.

These documents have played a significant role in shaping American democracy and governance. They have been enacted to address systemic discrimination and inequality. They were serious measurable attempts to correct past wrongs, bridge unfair start-ups, and play "catch-up" on known poorly implemented past performances. They have helped to expand the rights and protections of marginalized communities, in the uniting of these States. They have helped to protect individual rights and liberties, promote freedom and democracy, and ensure that all Americans were treated equally under the law. When these promises are kept, and laws and rights are enforced equally amongst its citizens of color.   Again, we will have cause for celebration!

OTHER MAJOR POLICIES CREATED TO ELIMINATE DIVISIVENESS

Elijah Anderson wrote an article so filled with truth about what happens to provoke racist Black or White Americans in this society, we wanted to discuss it with you. Anderson states that "We are filled with emotions of jealousy and resentment toward each other.   We, Americans who do not use our faith or 'the golden rule' as a moral compass, don't always want to see prosperity and advancements in any Americans." Anderson claims that "It has led to an exhausting life for people of color—and it has led to the undoing of policies that have nurtured Black advancement."   He is referring to the Affirmative Action law that was just snatched away from so many disenfranchised people. The major opposition contended that this was "reversed discrimination." What is your contention or feeling about this argument?

ANDERSON's comments: "Affirmative ACTION had helped keep the racial unrest of the '60s from flaring up again. When the kin - baby mamas, uncles, aunts — of ghetto residents secure middle-class livelihoods, those ghetto relatives hear about it. This gives the young people who live there a modicum of hope that they might do the same. Hope takes the edge off distress and desperation; it lessens the incentives for people to loot and burn. I would only add, "and find reason to blame and hate."

Dr. Anderson continues, "…to talk about the benefits of Affirmative Action, but I sharpened and expanded my case, explaining that it not only had lifted many Black people out of the ghetto, but had been a weapon in the Cold War. When unaligned countries and former colonies were trying to decide which superpower to follow, it helped.

Back then, Democrats and some Republicans were united in believing that Affirmative Action, by demonstrating the country's commitment to racial justice and equality, helped project American greatness to the world.   But now we know the real deal as far as America's commitment stands."

I think this demands your attention…Your thoughts, Scholars?

SIMILAR LAWS TO HELP BRING PEOPLE IN CONTACT WITH EACH OTHER

Here are some policies and laws that are similar to Affirmative Action and aim to help African Americans and women get help with by being considered for better opportunities:

1. **Equal Employment Opportunity (EEO)**: This policy prohibits employment discrimination based on race, color, religion, sex, or national origin. It requires employers to take affirmative action to ensure that all individuals have an equal opportunity for employment, regardless of their race, color, religion, sex, or national origin.

2. **Executive Order 11246**: This order requires all government contractors and subcontractors to expand job opportunities for minorities and women. It also established the Office of Federal Contract Compliance (OFCC) to enforce the order.

3. **Preferential Employment Strategies**: These strategies involve affirmative action on behalf of a racial minority group when a person's minority race results in employment for which race is not otherwise a significant qualification.

America is not a utopian nation. It will not likely ever be in the minds of many people. Besides, we do not feel America can define utopia for everyone. What America can do, however, is share its blessings and resources more equitably, equally, and humanely. That has to continue to be the goal of our nation considering the variety and number of people in today's diverse society. Hate and racism from within can be as counterproductive and destructive as any threat by a foreign country or outside terroristic group. America must work hard at all levels of the government, at presenting herself as being fair and just to all of her citizens.

I believe when we love and value our country, we will take better care of its people, its climate, resources, and what it stands for as Americans, regardless of race or skin colors.

Name something you learned in this chapter to help you not to hate other Americans, regardless of their color.

____

____

____

____

____

____

CHAPTER 10

Not Everybody
"Hated Us Because We Were Black"

This was one of the saddest comments I remember hearing amongst our college-aged conferees at our regional NAACP meeting a couple of years ago. A student enrolled at a major PWI in Texas was sharing the frustrations she was experiencing on campus. "Dr. Branch, it seems like everybody hates us because we are Black! We do not understand how we can just be walking to classes, minding our own business and somebody will go out of their way to holler racist 'stuff' at us…hateful stuff… 'N&#+@*!!! Go back to Africa! You don't belong here! '…and other stuff like that.' It makes me sick, and I just want to hurt somebody!"

Many times, in different environments, young Black Americans (and other people of color), may feel this way. We understand, sympathize, and wish very badly that we could utter a magic word and make it disappear. How do you respond? How do you get rid of or react in a civil manner to that kind of' stuff? Even more heartbreaking is, many times when reported to "authority figures," no one is held accountable. "They don't even feel you," she shared tearfully.

I shared this conversation with one of our much younger associates. Her response was something we did not expect…Denise, (a fictious name of course) waved her hand frantically to be recognized to respond. (Denise looked like the type of person that might know a whole lot of "sailor" words to use).

Reluctantly, we allowed her to speak. In a very distinct, sophisticated, and calm voice she offered the following bit of information. It went something like this: "I think a lot of the pain, shame, and hard-core anger we feel is self-induced. It is partially because of the way we perceive ourselves or allow ourselves to receive verbal racial abuse. We know who we are. Really, that should be enough. But another thing we have to do is observe who is the messenger. We don't take the time to consider the source. When ignorance is speaking, try not to listen. If you must listen, do not place credibility to it!"

WOW! If we could just reason like that when "stuff" is happening! Most of us just can't be that calm, but you know she is right. I hate to say this as an old faith-based woman, but "I feel you!" And those experiences are felt and received in different ways by different people. Someone said in a workshop once… "It's kinda like a 'buzzard' just dropped his meal on your windshield! Another participant added, "or on you!" We gotchu,' okay? We have been in your place at one time or the other in our longevity of lived experiences. Many other Black Americans understand and want to continue, with your help, to make America a better place for you and the generations that follow. You sometimes feel anger, hurt, shame, "sorry-for-your-self," hatred, helpless and hopeless… all rolled into one! All of your emotions and more are rolled and riled up during these times. But think about it seriously, the enemy wanted to hurt you in this manner. YOU allow it to happen. It's your choice.

We want to encourage our young scholars to formally and intentionally, dismiss these types of overt racist messages from your mind and within your spirit. Remember "Denise's admonishment… We cannot let the words of an ignorant evil, meanspirited person define you! You, (or certainly someone more worthy 'and credible'), reserve the rights of your attention and the arousal of your emotions. You are better than that. It is not a good feeling. Take the "high road" as someone of former first lady, Michelle Obama, might advise. Listen to someone with principles, values, and character. Don't hang on to it. Let it go! It is wrong, racist, and should not happen. However, many Americans of color face these and other harrowing verbal experiences in America even today as we approach the Semiquincentennial. Many times, you must just consider the source and keep moving forward and upward!

A NEED TO HATE

For some people, there seems to just be a psychological, overwhelming, "down to the bone" need to hate! We don't know why, we don't know how, but "they just do!" It is a psychological urge and a tendency to strike out and hurt for no reason. Bullies find this satisfying behavior. Friends and associates of bullies find this to be satisfying behavior. Is it fun and satisfaction just to hurt someone? For no reason? Skin color? Who colored her/him? That is a good reason! You don't know who does the coloring… Let's talk!

The messages I want to send through the pages of this project is a practical one…, not all Whites "have a need to" hate all Blacks. Not all Blacks "have a need to" hate all Whites. We have to say that intentionally and matter-of-factly, in order to make sure there is no misunderstanding about our experiences of racism in America. We, as faith-based Believers, must follow up with actions to demonstrate our personal commitment against hate. It is important because, we sometimes, intentionally, or unintentionally, make the mistake of conveniently, lumping everyone in a group when there is something negative happening around us. (*That is the way they act…*; *Seen one, seen 'em all; etc.*)

On the other hand, if one person does something good or positive, we don't tend to use that same "logic." That is wrong, and it can breed hate and divisiveness. It is unfair to judge a group of people who might be the same color or race as an evil perpetrator, as being representative of one whole race. It is unfair, illogical, stereotyping, and can easily breed hatred between both groups. I don't want to teach anyone to hate. So again, please know… "some people have a need to hate, but some don't." It is evident in all races and skin colors. As faith-based law abiding eighty- year-old, I don't teach or promote hate.

LEADING CIVIL RIGHTS ORGANIZATIONS THAT MATTERED

I believe that all efforts, large and small, to move America toward her goals of uniting her diverse society and citizenship have mattered. They all, and others of like mind, have moved America into a better light of hope and promises of freedom as we move into our 2026 celebrations. To imagine what America might have looked like without them, is sort of scary. Some were more subtle in presentation, and some were more intense, vocal, and visible. However, every attempt to preach and teach against hate was (and continues to be) needed and appreciated. Many sacrifices and names we will never know or hear called in this life, were made, or given. I sincerely believe, they were chosen vessels by God to do His will.

There were several well-known Civil Rights organizations that were started with both Whites and Blacks working together, to combat racism. I, in teaching against hate and divisiveness, propose more focus in this area. Let's intentionally teach and demonstrate the actions of Americans working for a common good in our nation. Opposing groups of Americans were often witnessed and taught in our history classes. I want to focus on groups who worked together, in unity, to help unite these states of America. Even some of our most notorious leading politicians, civic leaders, fellow Believers, and others have questioned the need for diversity and inclusion lessons. Many of these leaders show similar expressions and attitudes of divisiveness and anti-diversity feelings and messages in their daily work. They do not teach nor demonstrate messages against hate. Their message is un-American.

PATRIOTIC AMERICANS, TEACHING AND WORKING AGAINST DIVISIVENESS FOR OUR NATION

However, these Americans, White and Black, were determined to help America to live up to the promises of equality amongst her diverse people. There were many local, small communities, yet dedicated civil rights groups formed all over America. "Everybody hated us because we were Black," teaches hate only if you decide to embrace the idea. Dismiss these worldly interruptions. Be determined to rid your mind of such nonproductive thoughts. I know that is easier said than done but try it anyway. Trust me. I feel ya'! I know that is a favorite saying of young people like you. Another favorite saying from a young author like some of you, Jiles Clark, Never Give Up! Stay vigilant! Stay encouraged and encourage others!

Here are more reasons to 'rise and build' as your ancestors did. Be determined to move forward. You don't know unless you are taught. Once you know, teach others. You can be taught formally and informally in reading and researching the work and people on these pages. Learn more about the lives of these Black and White

Americans who worked in unity on special projects to unite America. Together, and in unity, they wanted to help enforce equal rights for all, regardless of race or skin color. Here are some examples that I want to share with you to show Blacks and Whites working together in unity. They have made a positive impact and a patriotic difference in our nation. Think of what America might have looked like during the celebration of its Semiquincentennial had these efforts not come to past:

1. **The National Association for the Advancement of Colored People (NAACP)**: The NAACP was founded in 1909 by a group of Black and White American citizens. This organization was formed in the minds of three White Americans and shared with some of their friends of color. They were activists who wanted America to keep her promises to all her people. Seeking a solution to some of the intolerable racist acts that were being carried out in America at that time, this group thought, together, and in unity, they could make a difference. Among the first hopeful and courageous members were W. E. B. Du Bois, Mary White Ovington, William English Walling, Dr. Henry Moskowitz and Ida B. Wells. The organization's mission was to secure political, educational, social, and economic equality for all people and to eliminate racial discrimination in the uniting of America. Blacks and Whites together, in unity. They, Black and White Americans, fighting for the civil rights of all citizens, formed the NAACP.

2. **The Congress of Racial Equality (CORE)**: CORE was founded in 1942 by an interracial group of students in Chicago. CORE founders were young American citizens who tried to unite, Black and White, to rid our nation of hate and divisiveness. They believed that through their respective

local chapters' public displays of interracial solidarity they could help make a difference. They hoped that their disciplined use of nonviolence could help to transform America into a truly colorblind democratic society. The organization's mission was to promote racial equality through nonviolent direct action. CORE played a significant role in the Civil Rights Movement, organizing sit-ins, freedom rides, and other protests. The original Freedom Ride of the 1960s were carried out by thirteen brave and courageous Americans, Black and White, women and men.

Together, and in unity, they headed south from Washington, D.C. These Civil Rights leaders braved the "known and the unknown" together, and in unity as young Americans, to take part in the original Freedom Rides. Many others followed later throughout the south. Though the Supreme Court had ruled it was unconstitutional to segregate public transportation, bus travel continued to be segregated across the South. And yes, there were proud patriotic White people who were members of the Congress of Racial Equality (CORE). Some young talented Americans, unfortunately, lost their lives during the Civil Rights Movement in the 1960s. Andrew Goodman and Michael Schwerner, both White, were CORE members who were killed by white supremacists, in Mississippi in 1964 while working to register Black voters. In unity, they were supporting a right of all American citizens. These are American history lessons that do not teach hate. This was another attempt to unite and work together to oppose hate and racism in America.

3. **The Student Nonviolent Coordinating Committee (SNCC)**: SNCC was founded in 1960 by a group of Black and White students. SNCC dedicated itself to organizing sit-ins, boycotts and other nonviolent action protests against

segregation and other forms of racial discrimination. SNCC began working to combat one of the most difficult issues of the Civil Rights Movement: the disenfranchisement of Black voters across the South through discriminatory voting laws, intimidation, and violence. These Black and White students participated, together, in sit-ins at segregated lunch counters in Greensboro, North Carolina and other parts of the South. They rode buses in mixed racial groups into areas known to hate Black and White groups who worked together. These brave young Black and White Americans worked tirelessly in an effort to help America to enforce equal rights in her diverse population.

Diane Nash, Joan Mulholland, and Michael Schwerner were a few names amongst the sit-in movement and founding members of SNCC. Together in unity, they helped America to serve its diverse population. Together, they helped organize the protests and recruit riders. Of course, they met lots of resistance and were called unscrupulous mean-spirited names. As freedom riders, they were met with violent and deadly resistance on the part of local law enforcement and white segregationists. Hundreds of them were arrested, beaten, and threatened with death. However, the Interstate Commerce Commission finally mandated the full desegregation of all interstate travel facilities, giving SNCC its first solid victory on a national level. Michael Schwerner, unfortunately, a brave White American, met his demise while on one of these American missions. He is one of our chosen vessels celebrated in Part III of this text.

Joan Mulholland still lives an activist life today. She stated in a Washington Post interview, "When I think about my role and the role of Whites in the Freedom Rides and the movement in general, I think things could certainly have changed without our participation. But I think it helped that I was White and a Southerner, because white segregationists saw other White Southerners taking a stand for change." I believe these are beautiful lessons from our history that does not teach our young Americans to hate. Our history can show another much-needed side as we move toward our Semiquincentennial. We must share more of this type of history lesson with our youth. These lessons are past-lived examples of unity against hate.

4. **The Southern Christian Leadership Conference (SCLC):** The SCLC was founded in 1957 by a group of Black and White ministers who followed their Christian life calling. Pastors James Reeb, Ralph Abernathy, Fred Shuttlesworth, Jonathan Daniel, and other clergy responded to their brother, Rev. Martin Luther King's call for help from the pulpits of America. Many answered this calling from Rev. King and a Higher Power. Viola Liuzzo was not a minister but worked tirelessly in the effort and works provided by the organization. She was, of course, one of the many. I wanted to share her story because in teaching against hate, we have to present "real life models."

Liuzzo was a real-life model of another White American who wanted to stand up for America and preach against hate. She was scrutinized by the FBI. She was ostracized by family and friends. She withstood it all. Unfortunately, she was killed at the hands of the Ku Klux Klan, as she, a young White American, tried to help Black people with voting rights. The SCLC organization's mission was to coordinate and support nonviolent protests against segregation and discrimination. Black and White Americans, together worked to make voting rights a reality in Mississippi and other states in America.

Unfortunately, at least three of its White members of this group were killed by racist White hate groups.   The SCLC organization preached against hate and divisiveness.   They fought fearlessly to help America live up to her promises to her diverse population.

In addition, I have listed five of the oldest established Black Women's organizations in America and a brief goal about each of their stated purposes:

1. **The Order of the Eastern Star** was founded in 1874. This is the oldest Black sorority-based women's organization in America. The organization's goal is to promote charity, truth, and loving-kindness among its members and to alleviate the suffering of others.

2. **The National Association of Colored Women's Clubs** was founded in 1896. This is the oldest African American secular organization in existence today. The organization's goal is to promote the welfare of women and children, to elevate the moral standards of the community, and to bring about civic betterment.

3. **The National Hook-Up of Black Women** was founded in 1974. This organization's goal is to empower women and their families through education, advocacy, and public policy.

4. **The National Council of Negro Women** was founded in 1935. This organization's goal is to advance opportunities and the quality of life for African American women, their families, and communities.

5. **The National Black Women's Health Project** was founded in 1983. This organization's goal is to improve the health and wellness of Black women and girls through education, advocacy, and public policy.

During the Civil Rights Era, several Black fraternities and sororities also played a significant role in fighting for racial equity and equality. Unlike the leading organizations previously mentioned, these organizations were formed to fill a special void. In some American settings, there was a blatant lack of inclusiveness practiced on the campuses that our ancestors helped to build. Racism and the color or fellow Americans' skin mattered to the point that Black people who wanted to be a part of a fraternity or a sorority could be denied admission. But these groups, as was the practice of our ancestors, created their own, persevered, and performed many community tasks on their own. Proudly, they took on the work to help make their communities better. When you research these organizations more thoroughly, you will find names of past members like Martin Luther King Jr, John Lewis, Thurgood Marshall, Mary Church Terrell, and Bayard Rustin. All were appreciated for their contributions.

Listed here are a few of those Black fraternities and sororities that worked together, to support and aid in the movement:

1. **Alpha Phi Alpha Fraternity, 1906**
2. **Alpha Kappa Alpha Sorority, 1908**
3 **Kappa Alpha Psi. 1911**
4. **Omega Psi Phi Fraternity, 1911**
5. **Delta Sigma Theta, 1913**
6. **Phi Beta Sigma, 1914**
7. **Zeta Phi Beta Sorority, 1920**
8. **Sigma Gamma Rho Sorority, 1922**
9. **Iota Phi Theta Fraternity, 1963**

As a Black race, we have always been proud and supportive of our Black Greek letter organizations. Most of these were started between 1906 and 1963. They have a rich history of community activism, benevolence, and non-profit support down through the years. There are many others who have made great contributions as well. I never had the privilege in college of being accepted into a sorority; I admit I have not always understood some of their past actions toward each other. Hopefully, none of this type of behavior is condoned or practiced anywhere today…especially the need for initiations and social orientations that involved brutality and "fun" violence. Hurting someone, even in a joking manner, is questionable for me. I admit I may have anachronistic values and thoughts, but to inflict pain intentionally is inexcusable, always.

Some, I have heard, were ruthless and mean-spirited toward pledges for various and sundry reasons. ALL of these fine organizations have made me proud as a mother, grandmother, and even great-grandmother. And I already know it isn't all groups, but for the few…like bad apples, and bad policemen…? Why so much brutality during your initiations? Why would you force a young brother or sister to drink alcohol or other concoctions to the point of embarrassing themselves (or others)? Could they have been better fraternity brothers or better sorority sisters if they had memorized Frederick Douglass's "What to The Slave Is The Fourth of July," or recited the "Gettysburg Address" by Abe Lincoln? Sung all three lyrics of James Weldon Johnson's "Lift Every Voice and Sing"? Recited Psalms 23, 24 and 37 1-27, or 1-33? I am just saying…Why?

Name something you learned in this chapter to help you not to hate other Americans, regardless of their color.

____

____

____

____

CHAPTER 11

Equality, Justice, and Human Rights for All American Citizens

During the Civil Rights Era, many White American heroes, sheroes, and organizations united and fought alongside our Black ancestors. In unity, together, they struggled to help our nation live up to promises of equality, justice, and human rights for all American citizens.

We, as Americans of all races and colors, can draw inspiration from these faith-based reminders of today and yesterday. Our ancestors, Black and White, have tried over and over to promote human rights and liberties, regardless of color. Unfortunately, they were usually in the minority, but it was their desire for our nation. To teach against hate, we must teach this, as well, to our children.

Our past mattered! but our present matters even more!! Racism, hatred, bigotry, divisiveness should be oxymorons when we enter any discussions showcasing or highlighting America. Freedom, liberty, emancipation, love, unity, and opportunity should be the buzz words we take into the conversations surrounding our Semiquincentennial year of celebrations! Hope, respect, Constitutional laws, principles, values, character, responsibility, and motivation to do good to other Americans, regardless of color, should be our goal. Lucky for our readers, we can begin or continue the conversation right here!

A SOLID FOUNDATION FOR SUPPORT

The Quakers' church group spoke out courageously in opposition of any man "owning" another man. They, along with others, created the Society of Friends. This group organized to promote and pushed the idea that all humans are equal. Because some saw the possibilities of America's waste in the misuse and mismanagement of talents and skills of Africans in America, they helped to provide funding for schooling in New York for freed Black people as far back as the 1780's. Their close lived experiences and close association with our ancestors, even as slaves, taught many Whites that Blacks were not "ignorant and unteachable." Our ancestors came with knowledge of mathematics, sciences, agriculture, herbalism, and they spoke other languages. Many White Americans knew our African ancestors could very well be a benefit to themselves and to America.

John Brown was such a man…an abolitionist who gave his life fighting slavery. Unlike Martin Luther King, Jr., who taught nonviolence, John Brown and his sons believed the only success that America would have against the riddance of slavery would be through violence. He, of course, led the infamous Harper Ferry raid. He was not seen as an American hero by many and was hung for his efforts to help the enslaved by these means. In elementary school, we were taught a playful little *jingle* or singing rhyme: John Brown's Body Lies a Moldin'(mouldering) In the Ground (grave}! Moldin' in the ground! Moldin' in the ground! His truth (soul) is marching on!

We were not taught the history behind the song, nor the main character's role in the song. But, John, Owen and his entire White family hated slavery and spent their lifetime fighting it. (We were not taught that part as elementary or high school students). Instead, we were led to believe "White people did not approve of the races being with each other." However, the Browns befriended Harriet Tubman and offered their home as a safe haven for escaping slaves heading North. The Browns became an intricate part of the Underground Railroad for run-a-way slaves seeking shelter to hide, rest and continue their tedious and dangerous journey.

This of course occurred at significant risk for Mr. Brown, his family, and the escapees. His bravery showed he was willing to collaborate with African Americans in an effort that, together, they could make a difference. He was White and he did not hate Black people due to their race or skin color. Harriet Tubman was Black. The slaves were Black. They did not hate Owen because of his race or his skin color. They welcomed the efforts and great brave contributions that were made on their behalf to try to make things better for fellow Americans. He and Harriet Tubman worked tirelessly on this project. Together, Black and White, they tried to make a difference. They were successful in that many slaves were able to escape into less hostile and friendlier territory.

WE MUST BE CAREFULLY TAUGHT...

There were many other brave, patriotic, and courageous White Americans who worked, harmoniously, and at risk of other Whites. We must teach our American youth of all races, intentionally, specifically, about these lived heroes and sheroes, and the choices they made in a multicultural society. We must remember Dr. Opal Lee's admonishment about the need to teach love. We must remind ourselves, and our generations to follow, about the lyrics from the

Roger and Hammerstein musical, *South Pacific*, "We Must Be Carefully Taught to Hate." We want to carefully teach against hatred, divisiveness, and every evil force that teaches us to become enemies. We are Americans. One Black and one White. We have many Brown friends and other colors, races, and groups. We are all proud Americans.

There are many great powerful examples of unsung heroes, sheroes, and role models from our ancestors' past. Their lives can be used to display and demonstrate the type of American spirit of freedom and liberties our ancestors, Black and White, wanted for Americans. We just need to be more inclusive, expansive, and focused on the best of our history, as well, in our teachings. We can use more demonstrations of the lives of races working in unity and against hate. Presenting the truth about all of these citizens of our country must become a reality. Valuable human social contributions to model the goals and objectives of our nation must be made. We must focus on making sure our teachings will support America's goals to show the uniting of our states and people in America, and what she stands for in the world.

Not all White Americans hated Black people, even in the most evil, dreadful, dark, and despicable portion of our history. Not every Black American hated White people due to the color of their skin, or lack thereof. Every Black hated racism and they hated all of the hideous abuse inflicted upon them and their families, due to their race. They had absolutely no control over being born into the Black race. Our Supreme Being and loving God was in full control of that blessing! No one had control over their birth. What we can control is how we treat people, of course, once they are here in America.

INFORMAL AND FORMAL LEARNING EXPERIENCES

White concerned citizens have stated specific reasons of how they were helped to become more race conscious. In our conversations and dialogue in different settings most have shared through a variety of ways. Discussions, conversations, civil debates on racial misrepresentation, and witnessing racial disparities between Blacks and Whites in the news media have all been cited as helpful. These incidental exposures: (talk shows, podcasts, etc.) have opened their eyes to understanding more about the racial realities in America. The media newscasts especially present the rigors as they really are and as they are happening in real time. No story book or hidden characters or make-believe stuff is needed. Some of the real happenings are unbelievable! Up until these things occurred in the news media, most Whites said they just never thought much about racism in America. Most could not verbalize specific reasons *not to do so.* They really did not have any reasons *to do so.* As African Americans, it is not always a search, it is just reality. It is not a stretch to understand, it is a lived experience.

COMMITTED TO MAKING AMERICA A FREEDOM LOVING NATION

I choose to intentionally begin this conversation with a concerted effort to provide a faith-based and educational push toward that effort. As we approach the 250th birthday of a nation that we believe was founded and established on Constitutional laws and principles of freedom, let's not pretend we can forget the shameful, embarrassing, weak minded atrocities of the past. Not reading, writing, or talking about these events will erase them? I don't think so. It does not promote and reflect the thoughts and promises of the foundation of freedoms established by our founding documents. As mature young American scholars, we can discuss the fact that in an effort to form a more perfect union, many lives were lost…not just Black people, but our brave and courageous White brothers who tried to help assure their Black brothers that America would keep its promises to all its people.

Our Black and White ancestors' lives were committed to making America a better world… Many gave their lives to defend our democracy and what it stood for as a leader in a free world. White sympathizers, abolitionists, morally sound faith-based Believers in America's Constitution and promises of equality and civil rights of every American, has always existed. We have not given a total picture when we omit some of the parts of our history and are selective in the parts given. We must be prepared to move forward openly and honestly. Great organization like the National Advancement for Colored People (NAACP), Student Nonviolent Coordinator Center, (SNCC), the Southern Christian Leadership Conference (SCLC), and the Congress for Racial Equality (CORE) were started with groups of Black and White Americans working together. They were American citizens who loved their country and wanted to try to make it better. They wanted to help America to make fair equitable laws and enforce them equally amongst her diverse population. Many of the names have not been called recognizing those Americans who loved this country, its diverse population, our Constitution and what it stood for. We don't teach this to our youth. *Why?* They have been marked absent from the many classroom curriculums and teachings of our classes on American History, African American History, and Government!

Even during our Black History celebration days and months, limited recognition of these great American contributions was diminished. Their labor and sacrifices have been dismissed, concealed, or forgotten. Their names have been lost in the discussions of great Americans. Many of these citizens were courageous enough to take an unpopular stand for the promises to "We, the People" in our country. Yet, they, too, fought for their newly founded country's representation in the world's arena as a land of liberty and the free!

So, even though they were in the minority, they fought with valor and patriotically for their American belief. Sometimes they fought alone, but many times the fight was along the side of their Black brothers and sisters. Their fight was for unity in the struggle for equal rights and protection under the laws instituted by America. Even though their beliefs were unpopular and indifferent from a small, but outspoken, powerful group of "egotistical bullies" and power-hungry men, these Americans demonstrated their commitment to the uniting of the States of America. Their togetherness, Black and White Americans, mattered. Their support for each other in the struggle mattered. They knew that it was the right thing to do for a country viewed by many as a proponent of freedom and liberty.

There were other White Americans who believed that racism, segregation, and other divisive practices were unacceptable in a democratic society. I think many more were bullied, threatened, and pressured into "going along to get along." Racism had no place in the idea of this country even at its inception. However, in defense of the ideas of the American democracy, these citizens were strong enough and committed enough to demonstrate personal courage and determination, to make a difference. Many chose different methods and paths to accomplish this task, but they were there! Together, they supported each other from America's inception, as our ancestors had been supporters, of the uniting of America. Some of the names included here marched and peacefully demonstrated their reckoning with America. They tried to help fellow Black Americans to gain the right to vote, own land, get jobs, go to school, buy homes, and live wherever they could afford. Black Americans wanted the same freedoms to eat in restaurants, lunch counters, go in the front door, sit in clean spacious waiting rooms, and other such places White fellow Americans, (and even known foreign white enemies) …could use.

For many Americans, as we approach the Semiquincentennial, it appears that a most lethal threat to the weakening and destruction of our democracy is from within. The continuous "thorn in the side" is the same as in the past 250 years… It is racism. Racism can and will dismantle these United States of America if it continues to run amuck in our beautiful country of diverse people. Americans must "bite the bullet," "step out of 'social and racial comfort' zones" and do something more promising and "noble" than banning history books.

Let's prepare to celebrate and commemorate the lives of these heroes and sheroes who fought vigilantly to bring America to this place at this time. There are way, way, too many to name in this setting. As you continue to research, you will learn even more unsung American citizens who worked and believed in our country and its promises. There are many scars, but we can begin healing with the truth. Nothing can be gained from lies, erasures, or abandonment. Our Black and White ancestors will be most proud of the truth.

Name something you learned in this chapter to help you not to hate other Americans, regardless of their color.

____

____

____

____

____

____

CHAPTER 12

Lest We Forget: White and Black American Sisters and Brothers in Unity, After Slavery

There are key important turning points to be remembered from the slavery era and during the Civil Rights Movement that followed. Just as with most national battles being fought, to make a real difference, there needs to be unity within its citizenship. When more whites became sympathizers and supporters of the human and civil rights causes and ideas, more Americans took notice. So, it is extremely important that Whites join in the fight when they know that hatred and divisive bullying, and inhumane treatment of citizens being discriminated against, due to race or skin color, occurs or has occurred. It is definitely true, historically, White intervention matters! It is definitely appreciated as well!

No matter how atrocious an incident was amongst African Americans… hangings, massacres, or evil doings … imposed upon innocent Black citizens, it was manifested as a greater horror when Whites were involved as victims. There was much more attention given to the matter at hand. A greater sense of urgency from politicians, Congress, the clergy, local, state, nationwide media attention and other such actions seem to unfold quicker and easier. Imagine what would have happened in America if the Leesburg Stockade girls had been White! We are not being racist in making that statement, that is America in the "raw"!   For many Whites, a very real eye opener to the evils of racism has been through some form of media…entertainment, as well as local, state, and national news. It, along with the use of cameras and cell phones, has helped in many respects, leading up to the 2026 celebrations.

Forms of bibliotherapy, formally and informally have helped to move the needle in a positive direction to help remove hate and racism in our society. We have heard that even the exposure of fictional characters like Attickus Finch in "To Kill a Mockingbird" is an example. The fact that many Whites have expressed that they were moved by the character's attachment to efforts to represent his client against racist behaviors and environment at all costs, was inspiring. This was the most impressive part of the book. Readers were moved by the White lawyer's fondness for his Black client. This is another way to teach against hate. The readers or observers in the movie received a visible lesson in rising above hate and malice toward others due to skin color or race. Many times, these are long-lasting lessons and deliver the same messages against hate, but in a nontoxic and entertaining manner.

According to some informal and formal research, innocent White Americans have stated specific reasons explaining how they were helped to become more conscious of racism and injustices in America. Often this has been through informal conversations, intentional debates, and racially focused presentations; as well as witnessing vicariously or in real time, racial incidents and disparities between Blacks and Whites. Others have cited observations of the excessive use of force directed at women of color, brutality and murders from persons seen on media, who were to provide protection and security, such as law enforcement.

Historically, and unfortunately, many of the heroes and sheroes of demonstrators, protestors, Freedom Riders, and others had to be seen as victims of malicious and deadly violence on videos and news media as well. The unsuspecting public just did not know the brutality inflicted on these citizens, Black and White, by some law enforcement officers. Not all officers were guilty, but enough that Black and some White families soon learned to have "the talk." This was especially true when Whites became victims. Whites realized this was true and some of them spoke out vehemently about the discrepancies and were even more determined to help make a difference. They fought against hate and for America and her promises. This was especially true, unfortunately, or fortunately, when White Americans were subjected to the hoses, police dogs, and other mean and atrocious opposition to what America stood for in the free world.

BLACKS CAN CHOOSE TO CELEBRATE WITH OUR WHITE AMERICAN SISTERS AND BROTHERS DURING AMERICA'S SEMIQUINCENTENNIAL

My older friends and I chose to intentionally begin this conversation with a concerted effort to preach against hate. I choose to teach against hate and divisiveness because our American population is so diverse, and it grows every day. I am on a mission to help unite these states in a diverse America! I want to provide a faith-based and educational push toward that effort to keep our democracy for another 250 years. I want to emphasize that our nation was purportedly established on a Christian foundation. Even though very few, if any, Christian principles, and values are practiced in our country today, I still have hope in the few. Unfortunately, even the practice of Sunday and weekly religious services are on the decline.

Loving our brothers as much as we love ourselves is not a priority. "Am I my brother's keeper?" has little relevancy inside or outside the churches in America. We are lacking in ridding our country of many sins - hate and divisiveness, seem to be two of them. We are a diverse society that becomes even more so on a daily basis. Yet, we are neglecting and denying preparations for these inevitable challenges in our homes, churches, schools, and other organizations in our workplace and communities. Our need for embracing inclusivity and togetherness that we must and should be intentionally teaching today is fading away under our watch. We must teach unity and togetherness, intentionally, to avoid unintentional informal incidental lessons of hate and divisiveness! I believe it should be a part of every American school's curriculum. Courses should be age and grade appropriate for K-12. Our young citizens must be carefully taught to fight against hate…because it is not an American idea!

In an effort to teach against racism, hatred, and divisiveness, we must teach truth as far as we know it. We must aim to be as impartial, inclusive, and impactful as possible, for as long as it takes.

To form a more perfect union, many lives must be involved and the contributions of many will need to be made. All races of a diverse population are important and must be recognized as valuable contributors. America has always been known as a melting pot and has tried to make a place for all of her people. But our nation's population has always faced opposition from small, powerful groups who have not chosen to embrace the "idea" of our America.

LEST WE FORGET: WHITE SISTERS AND BROTHERS...
IN UNITY

Over the years, many lives have been affected in America, "home of the free and land of the brave," by separation and biases among the diverse races. Sacrifices have been made, some more than others, lives were lost…not just Black people. But our brave and courageous White brothers who tried to help assure that America would keep its promises to all its people were noted, as well. They were committed to making America a better world, even giving their lives. They were defending our democracy and what it stood for then and today. It was the mission of Black and White Americans, and this must be taught to our young diverse citizens of today. If the young don't know, how can that become or continue to be a goal for our democracy? I believe these lessons should be taught in integrated settings. We must teach our young about the sacrifices made by all, to make our country better and more accepting of its diverse population.

White sympathizers, abolitionists, morally sound faith-based Believers in America's Constitution; and promises of equality and civil rights of every American have always existed. Their labor and sacrifices have been dismissed and concealed; their names have, sometimes, been lost in an effort to make sure we were heard. But in our discussions of White American ancestors, who were courageous enough to take an unpopular stand for the promises to "We, the People" of our country, we must remember to call their names. They have only received partial, limited recognition, or have somehow been ignored. Yet, they, too, fought for their newly founded country's representation in the world's arena as land of the free! They knew that a "free" life and one of enslavement given the lynching, beatings, and Jim Crow laws that many

Black people were subjected to in this free society called America, was evil and deficient. So, even though they were in the minority, they fought with valor and patriotically for their American beliefs that included us. Sometimes they fought alone and many times alongside their Black brothers and sisters in the struggle for equal rights and protection under the laws instituted by America. Their beliefs were unpopular and indifferent from a small, but powerful group of outspoken bullies and power-hungry men filled with hate. They knew the opposition shown against this faction was risky and dangerous for them, too, but many chose to take the risk anyway. As faith-based Believers and patriotic American citizens, they were willing to face the opposition. They were brutally beaten, ostracized, jailed and some paid the ultimate price. Most often it was at the hands of other Whites. They spoke out courageously, fearlessly, and at great risk to demonstrate against hate.

There were other Whites who believed that racism was unacceptable in a democratic society. Each helped in their own way. Often this was done in a covert way. All the help possible is needed to fight a raging beast like racism in a nonviolent pacifist manner. In defense of the ideals of American democracy, there is room for all. I welcome, still, those that are strong enough, fearless, and committed enough to demonstrate personal courage and determination to make a difference. Why? Because the struggle is still ongoing. The task of making our nation's promises a reality is still before us.

VOICES OF HOPE ARE LIFTING AND CLIMBING

Many White and Black Americans chose different paths to accomplish this task, but they were there, together, in unity, fighting for freedom, liberty and civil rights! Some marched as they tried to help fellow Black Americans to gain the right to vote, own land, get jobs, go to school, take vacations, and live wherever they could afford. Some marched so that they could dine in restaurants, eat at lunch counters, go in the front door, sit in waiting rooms where other citizens sat, and other such places that White America, (and even known foreign war enemies) …could be a part of… See how moronic and idiotic racism" running rampant and unchecked "can make a mockery of a united nation?"

Name something you learned in this chapter to help you not to hate other Americans, regardless of their color.

____

____

____

____

____

____

____

____

____

____

____

____

CHAPTER 13

The Semiquincentennial Matters to All Americans

During the time period, in the early 1900's thru the 1960's, many ugly, unforgettable, shameful, and sinful historical acts of racism and hatred were displayed. The headlines of local, state, national and world news made our "American freedom loving" country look bad. Not just in America, but all over the world our violent and deadly unrest was a part of the newscasts. However, the media were just doing their job in keeping the public aware of what was happening in America. In fact, to a certain degree, it was the media who brought a positive awareness to the plight of the Civil Rights Movement. Segregationists in many of our United States in the South, including both local law enforcement and white supremacist groups like the Ku Klux Klan, met the influx of Black and White volunteers with "a solid wall of resistance." Many White Americans were in awe. Many Black Americans knew by radio and word of mouth because they did not own televisions at the beginning.

Violence and hatred should never have been seen as a part of the American dream at any point, but especially now when America was trying to reconstruct and recover from past mistakes. In the latter 50's and early 60's, by the end of the summer, many Black and White

Americans had been arrested and jailed. Hundreds of volunteers were beaten, dozens brutally injured, and at least three of these young Americans were murdered. Their legacy will live on in the hearts and minds of many as true American heroes. James Chaney, a local Black man, was killed. Michael Schwerner and Andrew Goodman were White men from New York who wanted to advance the cause for civil rights of all citizens. Each valued America enough that, together, they just wanted to make a difference. They were all heroes who fought against hate. I will discuss these great Americans in "Part 2."

OTHER VOICES OF HOPE AND HELP FOR A BETTER TOMORROW

Many innocent and naive White Americans have stated specific reasons of how they were helped to become more race conscious. It has not been because of hate as much as just not being involved. Other reasons have been cited in discussions, meetings, informal chats on the job, church, and community events. Often, this is through informal conversations, school debates on racial issues, witnessing racial disparities between Blacks and Whites, observations of brutality and murders from persons who were to provide protection and security and others. Historically, and perhaps, unfortunately, many of the heroes and sheroes of the 1960s Freedom Riders and other White American workers who were involved in the struggle, had to be seen as casualties on the news and videos. The unsuspecting public just did not know the extent of brutality and injurious harm that the protestors and demonstrators were subjected to while helping America to keep her promises to all citizens. Also, they were astonished to see much of the violence and brutality was dealt out by law enforcement officers in their efforts to control multiracial incidents and diverse crowds. Not all officers were guilty, but enough were involved that Black families learned early on to have "the talk"! But, when Whites were victims, there was usually even more of an outcry and a determination to rectify some of the racial unrest. It mattered when diversity and unity was being demonstrated and administered.

BLACK AMERICANS CAN CELEBRATE WITH OUR WHITE AMERICAN SISTERS AND BROTHERS DURING AMERICA'S SESQUINCENTENNIAL

In an effort to teach against racism, hatred, and divisiveness, we must teach truth as far as we know it. We must aim to be as impartial, inclusive, and impactful as possible, for as long as it takes. To form a more perfect union, many lives must be involved and the contributions of many will need to be made. It might be a little uncomfortable for some, but never confrontational. Our discussions should be non-toxic, and respect should be shown in every way. That should be expected and respected. All races of a diverse population are important and must be recognized as valuable contributors. America has always been known as a melting pot and has tried to make a place for all her people. She should never give up. Our ancestors would be proud.

ONE NATION, AMERICAN SISTERS AND BROTHERS, IN UNITY

Over the years, many lives have been affected in America, "home of the free and land of the brave," by separation and biases among the diverse races. Sacrifices have been made, some more than others, lives were lost…not just Black people. But our brave and courageous White brothers and sisters who tried to help assure that America would keep its promises to all its people were noted, as well. They were committed to making America a better world, even sacrificing their lives. To defend our democracy and what it stood for, we must teach our young about the sacrifices made by all. It helps to rid America of hate and divisiveness.

White sympathizers, abolitionists, morally sound, faith-based Believers in America's Constitution and promises of equality and civil rights for every American have always existed. Their labor and sacrifices have been dismissed and concealed, their names have, sometimes, been lost or omitted in discussions of Americans who were courageous enough to take an unpopular stand for the promises to "We, the People" our country. They have only received partial, limited recognition, or have been ignored. Yet, they, too, fought for their newly founded country's representation in the world's arena as land of the free! They knew that a "free" life and one of enslavement, given the lynching, beatings, and Jim Crow laws that many Black people were subjected to in this free society called America, was evil and deficient.

So, even though they were in the minority, they fought with valor and patriotically for their American beliefs. Sometimes they fought alone and many times alongside their Black brothers and sisters in the struggle for equal rights and protection under the laws instituted by America. Their beliefs were unpopular and indifferent from a small, but powerful group of outspoken bullies and power-hungry men filled with hate. They knew the opposition shown was risky and dangerous for them, too, but many chose to take the risk anyway. As faith-based Believers and patriotic American citizens, they were willing to face the opposition. They spoke out and demonstrated against hate.

There were other White Americans who believed that racism was unacceptable in a democratic society. In defense of the ideals of American democracy, they were strong enough, fearless, and committed enough to demonstrate personal courage and determination to make a difference.

KING CALLED ON HIS BROTHERS OF THE CLOTH

Martin Luther King, Jr. sought the support of fellow White clergy to aid in the struggle of Civil Rights in America. He knew he could not handle such a humongous task alone. A few responded to his call as Brethren in the Ministry. They knew, just as King and his associates did, there was significant risk involved. They knew the buildup of racial hatred and rage among the opposition and resistance to change was real. Unfortunately, Whites and Blacks paid with their lives at the hands of other whites who did not support America's stated mission and pledges to the United States of America, and to the Republic for which it [stood]…

Some White and a few Black clergy were outspoken critics of Dr King and his efforts to seek freedom and civil rights for himself and other Americans. They called him a "communist," "troublemaker," "attention grabber," "jack leg preacher," "hustler" and a lot of other uncomplimentary names that 'haters' use. They did not see him as their brother and a man of God. There were many opponents who refused to abide by their own American laws and Biblical teachings. They were determined to disobey laws to allow Black Americans the same equal rights and freedoms White Americans enjoyed. They did not want to change the system of segregation and oppression with "liberty and justice for all." The opportunities to be gained from submissiveness and enslavement were too appealing to these "men of the cloth." Some were too fearful of white supremacists and the loss of worshippers and that kept them silent. The Gospel they had preached was not strong and meaningful enough to move them out of their safe places and comfort zones.

Many of them were sympathizers who feared the consequences. History tells us, that "most of the Southern White church leaders stayed on the sidelines and were complicit in White resistance."

They evidently were afraid of losing their churches' support or even fearing for their lives. They knew that the other side of hate was mean, vicious, and powerful in America. Many times, law enforcement was part of the violent groups and provided no protection for the victims. Our Black ancestors had no choice except to keep moving forward…That is exactly what they did.

A few White clergy, however, were supportive and recognized the need to change the sinful inhumane and brutal system of the remnants of slavery, Jim Crow, and segregation in the Southern states, in particular. So, they answered this calling; and they marched, protested, faced violence, and were willing to pay the price, no matter.

They knew that the consequences could be dire for their families as well. The sin of racism does not respect "men of the cloth." History supports the fact that some of these brutal beatings and deadly terroristic attacks were law enforcement men who knew these were nonviolent protesters. Some of the murderers of Black and White victims knew that they were clergy. But like most hate and sin, there is no respect for preachers or ministers, or the Gospel messages that they offered against hate.

For many Americans, as we approach the Semiquincentennial, the most troubling threat to the destruction of our democracy is racism and hate running rampant in our society. Racism can and will, while continuing to run rampant and unchecked, dismantle these diverse United States of America. There will be few winners, regardless of which side is chosen. That is another reason to promote UNITY in our democracy. If we love our country, we should be willing to fight TOGETHER to erase divisiveness. We can, and we must!

Name something you learned in this chapter to help you not to hate other Americans, regardless of their color.

CHAPTER 14

The Americans Who Did
Not Choose to Come, But Chose to Stay

Even our ancestors, in slavery times, caught the grandiose vision of the possibilities in the New World and the American dream beyond slavery. If America intended to keep her promises, there would be much to gain for America's newly freed citizens, and their offsprings. Though they had faced tough times, they had overcome the harsh adversities of major portions of slavery. Freedom had so much to offer to them and their descendants. They had opportunities to leave America and return to their respective countries on the African continent or respective islands. But, just like most White Americans who had faced hard times and did not choose to leave, Black Americans made that same decision. It was said that they felt no more interest in going back to Africa, than disillusioned Whites felt in going back to England, Ireland, Germany, or their other known countries of origin. They wanted to continue to build right here, granted under much duress, in the land, America. They wanted to share what America stood for in its Declaration of Independence, Constitution, and Amendments, and the promises of a free world.

I believe that this is a major reason more African American ancestors did not choose to "go back to Africa." (This is another familiar phrase and rant used toward Black people by racist whites during verbal confrontations). A few Black Americans did go back to reside on the continent. Many of the smarter ones, I believe, stayed. I think their rationale is praiseworthy.

When slavery ended in America, many of our ancestors had become very familiar with the American way of life for Whites, even though they (nor their offsprings) did not have all nor most of the privileges or opportunities to partake of it. My Dad used to say, "they worked aroun' it." Bottom line is they liked what they saw in their slave owners' homes, dresses, entertainment, businesses, job opportunities, leisure and recreation times, and other actions that made up the American lifestyle, devoid of the indignities of enslavement. They watched their masters' children grow up and go away to boarding schools, colleges, and universities. Of course, they dreamed of these same things for themselves and their children. They were humans! They were Americanized!

That is why the vision and dreams of Emancipation, Civil Rights and other freedom movements meant so much for so long and for so many Black people seeking equal and equitable rights to enjoy America. They had worked on the plantations and cleaned the nice huge Antebellum homes. They knew what life and wealth could bring from the inside and outside. Their skin color had not caused them to not be able to imagine the same possibilities for themselves. America would need to enforce the laws of freedom and protection they had proposed, of course. They were not afraid of hard labor. After slavery ended, they were supposed to be paid for some of that time in reparations (just as many Southern white plantation owners had received, as governmental assistance for emancipating their slaves). This was appealing, as well. They would now have this same opportunity and equal rights to acquire these amenities. After all, they helped to build schools, medical facilities, and other industries and institutions in America.

They thought there were noble purposes and benefits for them in their new world. Our ancestors wanted to experience the use and rewards of these facilities too. They dreamed of this freedom for their offsprings and descendants, as well. They wanted the freedom to partake in these same business opportunities. They wanted access to the same amount of funds to build nice homes and live in nice neighborhoods. They wanted opportunities to use their skills, talents, to invest, financially, in their families and explore the possibilities American Whites were enjoying. And there were high expectations amongst all Americans that there was even more to come. This was appealing. If the laws of protection of America's promises to her people would have been enforced equally, America was an ideal place to be. *Why leave? Why not stay?*

So, as fate would have it, fortunately or unfortunately, many of our Black ancestors chose to stay in America. This was as much their home as it was for anyone else who had worked the land for centuries. They felt no more ties to the continent of Africa than their masters did by returning to their past homelands. So, most chose to stay, and they continued to hope that America would keep her promises. The opportunities and rewards in the new nation would be offered eventually to all of her citizens. They did not participate in uprisings to leave or abandon America in violent clashes or by peaceful suggestions. This was the only country they knew. They grew to love America, geographically, as well as its freedom, "idea," and goals, in spite of the previous adversities. Our ancestors chose to stay because they believed in the American dream and promises to her citizens.

DISAPPOINTMENTS FOLLOWED BY HOPE

My friends and I believe that our ancestors wanted and expected to continue to give back to America. Among other blessings and challenges that America had to offer was an opportunity to work and raise their families as other law-abiding citizens were able to do.

They wanted and expected law and order. They wanted and expected it to be dealt with equally and provided for them when they were in need, as well as other Americans. They wanted to continue to rise and build. One of their greatest hopes was to belong and be treated as other Americans who were law abiding citizens. This did not happen to newly freed slaves, nor for many years thereafter. There was very little unity, equality, law enforcement or protection from those who were filled with hate, bigotry, and immoral acts against this group of God's creation. Many Black Americans tried to work and make their lives better, but they were not given an equal chance. Their pleas for help to advance and recover from violence and other vestiges of slavery and its wretched surrounding mentality, went unanswered.

They wanted to make it on their own as citizens who could participate in the American society. They felt, down through the years, that they had more to contribute to America. They wanted to belong and make America a 'sweet land of liberty' for all law-abiding citizens.

They, in slavery times, like Martin Luther King, during the Civil Rights era, did not ask for a FREE ride. Our ancestors asked for equal rights! Give me the same as other citizens! My children and I want the same protection of the law! To paraphrase… Treat me, according to the contents of my character, not the color of my skin. I can choose my character. I can thrive in a society like this one. Besides, we have paid our dues through our free labor. No need to go back now. If

America keeps her promises, we can continue to make this place a better place for both of us to enjoy!

Consequently, many of our Black and White ancestors did not participate in insurrections like the Harper's Ferry attack (though both races were there). They did not participate in the Liberia Movement and other attempts to make their lives better on a different continent.   While many felt totally overpowered and helpless, there was always a faction that never gave up hope. They hoped they would survive and become a part of the America they had helped to build.   In spite of the adversities, broken promises, and unequal treatments dealt with, there was still hope that things would get better for them and the next generations. Then, just as now, we have always needed to, as nationally renowned Civil Rights Leader and Advocate, Reverend Jesse Jackson taught, Keep Hope Alive! Unfortunately, there have been many disappointing times. However, we, as a group of strong resilient people have continued to thrive and keep hope alive. We have chosen to stay and continue to help America achieve her goals and promises to all of her people.

Why Black people have constantly been denied full citizenship in a country they helped to build "for FREE" is troubling and puzzling! In America, our native land, this is unfair, unpatriotic, and unlawful. It will always be a part of our mission, hopes, and dreams to overcome.   We must encourage others to keep hope alive, as well. We must continue to learn, teach, promote, and model unity and togetherness between Black Americans and White Americans in order to achieve our ancestors wishes.

Divisiveness between the races, has always been a major problem since the inception of these United States. We never witnessed other marginalized groups that were discriminated against in the same overt and blatant manner as this group. For example, while growing up, I was never asked to drink from a certain water fountain because I was a woman or female. But there were signs that distinctively kept me separated from White races.

White women have been discriminated against because of their gender, but there is little or no comparison to the discrimination dealt out to Black women. There were no blatant signs opposing White women, LGBTQ+, or other marginalized groups; but for centuries, including this one, we as a people were faced with them. No Blacks or White Only signs often greeted me. They were over water fountains, restroom doors, waiting rooms, dining areas, and many other areas where White Americans, from both of these groups, used frequently and freely.

I remember, one day, wanting to use the library in my, then, hometown of Atlanta, Texas, to do a research paper. I was a teacher working on my Master's degree! I was a professional law-abiding citizen (in my mind)! Yet, I was denied. Other marginalized groups had access, but Black people did not, even when trying to "improve their lot in life !"

On another occasion, our dryer broke down and I had seen this raggedy looking washeteria about a mile up the highway from our home. When I pulled into the parking lot, with a basket of wet clothes and my toddler, James Jr. in tow, I got a dose of Jim Crow again. All of the times I had passed there in the past, I had missed this huge dirty WHITE ONLY sign in the window. I will let you guess if I dried my clothes in this dirty filthy place, or if I came home and cried. *Which would you have done?* I also made up my mind, I had to leave Atlanta, Texas as soon as possible!

There are many other stories of lived experiences that I, and most other seventy and eighty plus year olds can share with you. Try talking to your oldest family member at your next family reunion! It could be an amazing experience, I assure you! No need to only read books. *After all, we are the researched – we represent history - and a conversation with us could be a benefit to you!* I have experienced this kind of "Americanism' and more! But we don't have to teach hate because of it. My faith and hope in a brighter future, more than, perhaps, other experiences in life, kept me moving forward. That is my major purpose in sharing these belittling, but true messages with you.

For centuries, Black males and females, have been denied their rightful place as citizens in America. That can and must change. We, as descendants of White and Black Americans are determined to see our country become strong enough to keep her promises. We don't want others to leave because of the lack of an equal and fair society, and we have also chosen to stay. These examples are from our shameful past, and from most of the incidents that have shown improvement over the years. It has taken that long because of continuous racist impositions and practices that are still evident in our society. It continues to get better. Such racist overt divisiveness as seen in waiting areas, eating establishments, entertainment venues, etc., but you need to be aware of where hatred and racism is capable of going. It exists systemically and covertly in many mean and despicable ways. The mindset of bigotry and hate has no limits. (Read and research the story included here about the Leesburg girls who wanted to see a movie in their hometown down in Georgia.). It appears almost as innocent while happening, as the expectations rendered, or accountability issued afterwards.

Our forefathers' and mothers' greatest hope was to overcome these obstacles and become FREE American citizens (as well as their descendants) in a land promoting the ideas of equal rights. They looked forward to escaping poverty and welfare, share cropping, using the same or equal tools for success given to other Americans. They wanted to be allowed to enjoy the same equal rights, enforcement, and protection of laws. The same equal job opportunities, and the same liberty and freedoms America promised to all citizens were expected and sought. Our ancestors wanted to enjoy the freedom to vote, worship, live wherever they could afford, get jobs they were qualified to handle and enjoy other good things around them.

They wanted and expected equal enactment and protection under local, state, and Federal laws for all citizens. They wanted to earn their own way: equal pay and income and buy homes, and work their own land, food, clothing, supplies and goods. Our ancestors hoped that they (and their descendants) too, could find that in America, the "land of the free and the home of the brave." If our new nation's promises were kept, together, in unity, we would one day be able to go to the same schools, colleges, camps, hotels, restaurants, and many other places that they played major roles in building! So, they chose to stay.

HOPE FOR NO MORE STEROTYPYING AND MONOLITHIC GROUPING FROM DAYS PAST

They did not lose hope that in the future, our Black generations of young Americans would enjoy being held accountable for their character as opposed to monolithic negative judgment received due to race and skin color. This American example or model as a Democratic society's pledge, with all its amenities, was a great model if every citizen would be allowed to exercise and be afforded these equal opportunities.

Our founders wrote beautiful freedom-loving words and promises, but America was not committed to enforcing her own laws equally.

She never fully kept her promises to our race and to other people of color. This has been a real issue in America for over 250 years. Many have wondered why we chose to stay. Leading into the Semiquincentennial many consider our history of racism an embarrassing blight on our past. Some view our history as an opportunity to help future generations rise above this inhumane asinine thinking. The Declaration of Independence, the Emancipation Proclamation, Amendments, and various Civil Rights acts have offered excellent attempts at making shameful acts of racist divisive actions committed by immoral power-hungry people, disappear. Over the years, such ideal and worthy efforts have been promised and offered as meaningful solutions toward moving toward the freedom of African Americans. But the actions, enforcement, and consistent support of these promises have yet to be fulfilled in a way that is equal and equitable. But many Americans believe it is never too late to begin this journey and so we have proudly claimed America as our home.

Years ago, I viewed the first nationally televised MLK speech on my black and white television screen. (Of course, the antennas had to be adjusted for a more precise view). But seriously, I, like others of that time, read it in print and played it over and over in my mind. For me, it was very moving, relevant, and got a lot of shouts of "amens." For me, as an African American Believer, the speech acknowledges what was wrong with our country, but encouraged us as a race to not give up. Dr. King wanted us to continue to have hope. His speeches are very emotionally charged, yet they remain uplifting for our old and young, celebratory and weary spirits, even today. Dr. Martin Luther King pointed this out in his inspiring "I Have a Dream" speech. He stated that "the country's founders had signed a promissory note that offered great freedom and opportunity…but, instead of honoring this sacred obligation, America has given the Negro people a bad check, a check which has come back marked insufficient funds." We think he was correct in these observations, aka "accusations."

So, here we are getting ready for the great Semiquincentennial celebration in 2026. Most of the great laws to promote and celebrate our country's freedom and equality have been present since 1776. Many of these laws are not real in the diverse segments of America's population. Great new protective amendments have been added. Practicing and enforcement have been a challenge and need to be mitigated now. Some changes will always occur, but it should never be at the expense of another person's freedom and rights related to diversity, race, and skin color. We must not keep making or dangling promises to our citizens, staged in political environments that we know we are not going to keep equally. Our country's past history is filled with helpful laws that were later called "reversed discrimination" and anything else imagined and concocted by Americans who were uncomfortable with racial progress and opportunities for people of color. Some of these decision-makers have sat in the highest of places in America. This type of recall on our progress to gain full citizenship has occurred through many generations. But we must keep trying to help America to enact and enforce her own expressed promises for "We the People…" We must find new resourceful ways of promoting and enacting them. The citizenry of this great country deserves this bit of respect, as well as this right. We continue to believe that our trust, unity, and togetherness must prevail. We must not accept racism and hate in our society and in this great democracy!

As we approach the next 250 years, our nation's future depends greatly on how well racism is managed in our diverse population of citizens. It has not been managed well. Yet, most Americans, White and Black, are optimistic about their future. We are still working to get equal voting rights. We are still fighting for social and equal justice in this country. Our parents still are afraid of police encounters, especially for their male youth. Redlining, overt and covert racist attacks can still be viewed in media daily. Affirmative Action has been snatched from under us. Our chances for positive change in a racist society must be implemented through laws of powerful non-racist law makers. Unfortunately, positive changes that are most needed in a diverse society are not birthed or enforced from the head (knowledge) nor the heart (kindness). Enforced laws are needed in America to erase much of the overt and covert acts of discrimination and bigotry paraded in America today.

Our history shows that all of this has happened before. After the Civil War, under the aegis of Reconstruction, Black people, fresh out of slavery, for a time became professionals, businessmen, and politicians. But when federal troops left the former Confederate states around 1877, and it appeared that a small, but powerful, group of white politicians in the South tried to reconstitute slavery with the long rule of Jim Crow, they were successful. Let this lesson alone be a warning as to how fast evil can spread if you are not mindful; and being monitored by federal laws is extremely important. You must assume full responsibility to continue to study your history. Learning about your past helps you to prepare for a better future.

Our ancestors had hopes and dreams, as patriotic law-abiding citizens, for freedom. They wanted to fully participate in the American dream for themselves and for their descendants. The overwhelming majority were denied this opportunity because they were born, lived, and died as slaves. But there were almost always enough determined and tenacious citizens that were capable, able, and allowed to move forward to keep hope alive.

I know personally, what it feels like to be denied access to eating places, lodging, libraries, movie theaters, schools, dormitories; riding on the back of the Greyhound and Trailway busses, etc. I am grateful that our country is too mature in her thinking to continue such moronic and asinine foolishness. However, a great amount of covert systemic racism is still "alive and well" within our great nation.

I lived thru this time of segregation; and through God's amazing grace and direction, it did not cause me to hate anyone. I hated the system imposed upon me by others who denied me the rights they enjoyed for themselves! *Why were we denied these privileges? Was it just because we were Black?* I never wanted my children to grow up in an "Atlanta, or Jacksonville, Texas," where they would face the same types of discrimination. I wanted them to be judged by the character that James Sr. and I had taught them.

Yet, we are not afraid or sorry for the choices our ancestors made centuries ago, to declare America as our home. "Lift Every Voice and Sing" remains an iconic theme that resonates in our hearts and minds. Its lyrics belong to us, as a race, and to our friends of other races, who have shared so much of themselves in the struggle for humankind. In the words of James Weldon Johnson, who by his own admission, "cried like a baby" as he penned these words…

"God of our weary years, God of our silent tears,
Thou who has brought us thus far on our way,
Thou who has by thy might, led us into the light,
Keep us forever in the path we pray."

Johnson, a Man of the Cloth, warned us as a race, of the importance of our duties as well…

"Lest our feet stray from the places our God where we met Thee,
Lest our hearts drunk with the wine of the world we forget Thee,
Shadowed beneath thy hand, May we forever stand,
True to our God, true to our native land!"

As we approach our nation's 250-year mark, and celebrations, is color still a problem for most Americans? We do not know, but we plan to keep trying to figure it out. Is this a natural part of nature…*we just have to hate anyone who is Black?* No, remember the lyrics in the song in the musical, South Pacific…we must be carefully taught!?

I agree, you must be carefully taught to hate. That is what racism is … it is hate, based on race. It is not always about color, but it is always a sinful part of mankind! We, as a Black race of Americans, did not choose to come, but through God's grace, guidance, mercy, and protection, we have chosen to stay. America is our "native land."

Name something you learned in this chapter to help you not to hate other Americans, regardless of their color.

____

____

____

____

____

____

____

____

____

____

PART 2

Vignettes of Early American White Heroes and Sheroes Who Struggled and Fought to Help Unite AMERICA During Slavery

Part 2 is dedicated to providing vignettes, or brief introductory information and names to follow up on, of Americans who chose not to separate, divide, or hate. We believe these represent only a few of the many who demonstrated a true love for a united America.

WHITE AND BLACK AMERICANS IN THE SLAVERY ERA STRUGGLE

From our nation's very beginning, many Black and White citizens saw a brighter future in a diverse nation of people, fresh ideas of inclusion, and equal rights for all human beings. These Americans were fearless in their desire to make a difference in providing equality to our nation's peoples.

They were creative, innovative, and sacrificial in choosing the varied platforms on which to perform their patriotic efforts. Many were neophytes, innocent, and, yes, some paid the ultimate price to help build an American nation strong enough to embrace all of her people, including those who were enslaved. They forfeited wealth, reputation, friends, and ultimately, their lives for 'the cause'." All are White American heroes and sheroes. We think of them as Chosen Vessels who were on a mission to serve God, our nation, and humanity.

I like sharing these names and brief bits of information about the lives and legacies of these great Americans. There are too many unsung heroes and sheroes to name in this format. They all believed in America then and what it stands for today.

In an effort to grapple with our history we want to prompt further research, discovery, and discussion. Here are a few vignettes from the Slavery Era to begin the discussions:

1. **William Lloyd Garrison** was born in 1805 and died in 1879. He was a wealthy and influential White American abolitionist, journalist, social reformer, and newspaper owner. He used his wealth, voice, and influence to speak out against this repugnant system of humanity, whenever and wherever he could. He devoted his life to fighting slavery. He, along with Black Abolitionist and friend, W.E B DuBois, formed The American

Anti-Slavery Society. Together and in unity, they fought against hate. The Society was formed in 1833. It advocated and promoted the cause of immediate abolition of slavery, as opposed to the gradual riddance as some had offered. It is said that in less than ten years, by 1840, its auxiliary societies numbered around 2,000, with a total membership ranging from 150,000 to 200,000. The Society sponsored meetings, adopted resolutions, signed antislavery petitions to be sent to Congress, published journals, and enlisted subscriptions, printed and distributed propaganda in vast quantities, and sent out agents and lecturers to carry the antislavery messages."

Garrison was best known as the owner of his widely read anti-slavery newspaper, *The Liberator*. He continued this influential work of publishing until slavery in the United States was abolished by the Thirteenth Amendment. *The Liberator* was widely circulated and had a significant impact on public opinion in the North.

Garrison's legacy and work as an abolitionist and social reformer played an important and necessary role in Whites forcefully speaking out in opposition to enslavement in these United States of America.

2. **Arthur and Lewis Tappan** were American businessmen, philanthropists, and abolitionists who financed anti-slavery movements. Arthur Tappan was born on May 22, 1786; he died on July 23, 1865. Lewis Tappan, his brother, was born May 23, 1788, and died on June 21, 1873.

The Tappan brothers were born in Northampton, Massachusetts into a religious, educated and wealthy family. Arthur moved to Boston at the age of 15 and established a dry goods business in

Portland, Maine in 1807. In 1826, he and his brother, Lewis, moved to New York City and established a silk importing business. The brothers were successful businessmen but viewed making money as "less important than saving souls." They founded the New York Journal of Commerce with Samuel Morse in 1827 and made it a publication free of "immoral advertisements." Arthur Tappan helped to found the American Anti-Slavery Society and served as its first president for almost 10 years, from 1833 to 1840. During his leadership, the society became prominent and well-known for publishing a large number of abolitionist pamphlets and almanacs.

The Tappans' philanthropic efforts and work toward abolishing slavery were not without controversy. Arthur's support for a proposal of a college for African Americans in New Haven led to the destruction of his summer home in Connecticut by a mob in 1831. Yet, he remained an influential American businessman, philanthropist, and abolitionist who used much of his energy and fortune in the struggle to help put an end to slavery. The brothers' efforts made a difference. Lewis Tappan was a New York abolitionist who worked to achieve freedom for the enslaved Africans aboard the Amistad. Arthur and Lewis Tappan were successful businessmen, but commerce was never their foremost interest. Their goal was to speak out adamantly against the evil system of slavery and the enslavement of other human beings. They also helped found Oberlin College, in Oberlin, Ohio, which admitted people of all races.

3. **John and Owen Brown Family offered safe houses to escaping slaves as underground railroad masters.** Born in Connecticut in 1800 and raised in Ohio, John Brown came from a staunchly Calvinist and anti-slavery family. He spent much of his life failing at a variety of businesses–he declared bankruptcy

in his early forties and had more than twenty lawsuits filed against him. In 1837, his life changed irrevocably when he attended an abolition meeting in Cleveland, during which he was so moved that he publicly announced his dedication to destroying the institution of slavery. As early as 1848, he was formulating a plan to incite an insurrection.

In October 1859, the U.S. military arsenal at Harpers Ferry was the target of an assault by an armed band of abolitionists led by John Brown. (Originally part of Virginia, Harpers Ferry. Potomac rivers.) The raid was intended to be the first stage in an elaborate plan to establish an independent stronghold of freed slaves in the mountains of Maryland and Virginia.

John Brown was captured during the raid and later convicted of treason and hanged. The raid inflamed white Southerners' fears of slave rebellions. It also increased the mounting tension between Northern and Southern states before the American Civil War (1861-65).

It is said that after decades of giving speeches to various groups and arguing against slavery, Brown began to lose his patience. Leading conversations and discussions to the wealthy and powerful began to lose its appeal. Brown began to dislike this pacifist approach. This type of "moral suasion," as mainstream abolitionist William Lloyd Garrison called it, was not producing the results he wanted to see. The "changing hearts and minds" or "changing the narrative" needed to be revisited. He had a true passion for his work as an abolitionist and soon adopted the mentality of "change by any means necessary."

Frederick Douglass once stated that Brown was "in sympathy, a

Black man… as though his own soul had been pierced with the iron of slavery." Before it was popular, Brown lived and worked alongside Black people.

W.E.B. Du Bois put it this way, Brown was "a companion to their daily life, knew their faults and virtues."

Novelist Richard Henry Dana met Brown and his family in North Elba, NY, in 1849. Even though he was an anti-slavery writer, he shared his amazement and shock to find Brown matter-of-factly introducing white and Black residents using titles, equally. "The man was 'Mr. Jefferson,' and the woman 'Mrs. Wait.'" Dana concluded, "It was plain this family acted on principles they expounded" This writer cautions that "Yet, John Brown remains better known for his violence than his inviolable wish, that the American society might renounce its covert war of 'two nations': White, and everyone else.

4. **Owen Brown** was born on November 4, 1824. He died on January 8, 1889. He was the third son of abolitionist John Brown. He participated more in his father's anti-slavery activities than did any of his siblings. He was also the son who joined his father in Chatham, Ontario, Canada, when the raid was planned; he was chosen as treasurer of the organization of which his father was made president. He described himself as "an engineer on the Underground Railroad." He was the only son to participate in the Bleeding Kansas activities. Unfortunately, in another act of violence, he killed a man during the encounter of the Pottawatomie massacre, He also contributed to his father's raid on Harpers Ferry. He was the only son of Brown present in Tabor, Iowa, when Brown's recruits were trained and drilled. This entire family, in spite of the violence, were known to be deeply religious and staunch supporters of ridding America of slavery.

5. **Elizabeth Heyrick** was born on December 4, 1769. She died on October 18, 1831. She was a philanthropist and campaigner against slavery. Heyrick supported immediate abolition of slavery rather than gradual abolition. Around 1824, she published a pamphlet entitled "Immediate, not Gradual Abolition." She used this communication to criticize leading anti-slavery campaigners, such as William Wilberforce, for their assumptions that the institution of slavery would gradually die out. She campaigned against the group for focusing too much time and effort on the slave trade. She wanted the system to be attacked and to have more progression toward ending this despicable act. Heyrick believed that women should be involved in these issues as they were qualified "not only to sympathize with suffering, but also to plead for the oppressed" in a stronger and more effective way.

Heyrick was a founding member of the Birmingham Ladies Society for the Relief of Negro Slaves in 1825. This was the first ladies' anti-slavery society in the world. She also encouraged a social movement to boycott sugar from the West Indies to promote more public awareness of the issues of the slave trade and hit the profits of planters and importers of slave-produced goods. She believed a boycott of these goods could speed up the abolishment of this social evil, slavery. She visited grocers' shops to persuade them not to stock them with this merchandise. She continued to rankle others as she openly showed sympathy with the revolts in the West Indies people. In one of her many pamphlets, she compared the previous British uprisings for their freedom against the Turks, with the slaves' uprisings against their masters. "Were the slaves only protecting themselves from the most degrading and intolerable oppression imagined?" she reasoned. She protested against slavery at significant risk to her life for what she believed was right.

Heyrick's legacy will live on in the minds of many. She received a glowing show of support from seventy new British women's' anti-slavery societies that sprang up after one of her most famous writings around 1824.

6. **Gerrit Smith** was born on March 6, 1797. He died on December 28, 1874. He was a White American abolitionist, social reformer, businessman, public intellectual, and philanthropist in New York.

Smith was a very wealthy landowner in his state. It is said that at one time he owned nearly 700,000 acres of land in the Adirondacks area of New York. From these land holdings, he established Timbuctoo, a settlement for Blacks in 1846 which is located in North Elba, New York. Smith divided 120,000 acres of land that he owned in the Adirondacks into 40-acre plots and granted thousands of deeds to Black families from around the state and country. The settlement was established to provide Black men with $250 worth of property. This amount of property value was the requirement for Black men to vote at that time.

Each of the new settlers were required to cultivate the land to improve its value and promote self-sufficiency. Cutting down evergreens, clearing rocks, and securing money to pay taxes on the land were a few of the many unexpected obstacles the new settlers faced. Although Smith's donation was praised by Frederick Douglass and other abolitionists, the settlers found the situation to be more than they could handle with limited resources. But Smith had tried to make it work.

He was an energetic politician as well. He was an unsuccessful candidate for President of the United States in 1848, 1856, and

1860. He did, however, serve a term in the House of Representatives from 1853 to 1854.

Smith's legacy will show he was committed to political reform and the elimination of slavery. He was a significant financial contributor to the Liberty Party and the Republican Party throughout his life. Smith's estate in Peterboro, New York was a hub for abolitionist activity. So many fugitive slaves came to Peterboro to ask for his help (usually, in reaching Canada) that there is a book about them.

He was the primary organizer of the only assembly of escaped slaves (as opposed to free Blacks) ever to meet in the United States. Historically, it was the Fugitive Slave Convention of 1850. It took place in neighboring Cazenovia because Peterboro was too small for the meeting. Smith was one of the Secret Six who financially supported John Brown's raid at Harpers Ferry in 1859. Brown's farm, in North Elba, was on land he bought from Smith.

7. **Warner Mifflin** was born in 1745. He died in -1798. He was a White American hero and abolitionist.

Warner Mifflin was born into a family of great wealth. He was an abolitionist who once owned slaves, which were a part of an inheritance. Mifflin's efforts were instrumental in raising awareness about the cruelty and injustices of slavery. He was initially hesitant to free his slaves but became convinced that owning them was sinful. A personal revelation caused him to fear damnation for his participation in slavery. Mifflin began freeing his own slaves in 1774 and convinced his father to do the same. He traveled extensively, giving speeches, and writing articles to educate people about the evils and horrors of the institution of slavery. Mifflin also played a crucial role in organizing anti-slavery societies and supporting legal challenges against slavery.

Mifflin was often involved in legal battles that challenged the legality of slaveholding. In 1780, he successfully sued for freedom on behalf of two enslaved individuals named Rachel and Hannah. This landmark case helped establish important legal precedents that undermined the institution of slavery. Mifflin freed twenty-two slaves and entered into free labor contracts with them to keep his work force intact. He provided schooling for their children. His examples inspired others to model his behavior. Mifflin traveled extensively to promote and encourage others to free their slaves, too.

Mifflin's commitment to nonviolence and his Quaker beliefs shaped his approach to activism. He believed in peaceful resistance and worked towards achieving change through moral persuasion, rather than violence or confrontation. A play entitled, "The Quaker Off of Mifflin," casting "Walter Mifflin" as the main character and hero, was also helpful in changing attitudes and reducing the slave population.

Warner Mifflin is remembered as a courageous abolitionist who fought tirelessly for justice and equality. He left a lasting legacy in the fight against slavery. He grew up with slaves as playmates; yet he became one of the earliest and most prominent advocates for the abolition of slavery in the United States. Mifflin believed that African Americans wanted nothing more than a level playing field to demonstrate their natural equality with White citizens. African Americans formed the African Warner Mifflin Society in the 19th century in honor of Mifflin.

8. **Prudence Crandall** was a White American abolitionist, educator, emancipator, and a human rights advocate. In 1833, she opened the first Black female academy, Miss Crandall's School for Young Ladies and Little Misses of Color, in Canterbury, Connecticut. This resulted in her being arrested and imprisoned for a brief period of time because it violated "the Black Law." (The law was intended to deter Crandall, and others, in her efforts to educate Black youth there). Four prominent white men, led by a white supremacist, Andrew Judson, attempted to convince Crandall that her school for young women of color would be detrimental to the safety of the white people in the town. Their stated beliefs of Black people: "they are an inferior race of beings, can never rise from their menial conditions in 'our' country and should never be recognized as the equals of the whites…" did not discourage her. They claimed that the boarding school would encourage thoughts of "social equality and intermarriage of whites and Blacks, to which she responded, according to court documents, "Moses had a Black wife." Determined, Crandall was arrested and placed in the county jail for one night—she refused to be bonded out. She wanted others in the American public to know she was being jailed and why. It was effective and caused outrage from many. The Vermont Chronicle newspaper reported it under the headline "Shame on Connecticut." The following day she was released on bond to await her trial.

Prudence Crandall's fight against this evil force of injustice was just beginning. Her efforts caused problems and alienated her amongst family and friends. In addition, under the Black Law, the townspeople offered no help or any amenities to the students or Crandall. Stagecoach drivers refused to provide transportation for them, the town doctors refused to treat them. Townspeople poisoned the school's well with animal feces and prevented

Crandall from obtaining water from other sources. Although she faced extreme difficulties, Crandall continued to fight to open her school to young women of color. At that point, this angered certain members of the community even more. As a result, Crandall's students suffered the indignity of the trial and the knowledge of feeling rejected. One 17-year-old young Black scholar was arrested for vagrancy. However, a local wealthy abolitionist, Samuel J. May, was able to post a bail bond. Approximately $10,000 was raised through collections and donations as well.

The opposition to Crandall's school soon turned even more violent with an attempt to set the building on fire, and an attack at night breaking all the windows. For her students' safety, she closed the school and left the state. After being harassed and attacked by a mob, she moved with her husband Reverend Calvin Philleo to Illinois. When he died in 1874, she and her brother moved to a farm near Elk Falls. Prudence taught throughout her long life and was an outspoken champion for equality of education, regardless of color, as well as for the rights of women.

Prudence Crandall's legacy lives on, even though the school was forced to close. She was a great American shero for many. She wanted to help these African American girls to become as successful as possible and tried to help America to become all that she could possibly be to those girls.

9. **Samuel J. May** (September 12, 1797 – July 1, 1871). was a White American reformer who fully supported the abolition of slavery, during the nineteenth century. Samuel graduated from Harvard Divinity School in 1820.

After experiencing the tragic loss of his brother, at an early age, he claimed the dreams he had following the fatal accident led him to devote his life to God. They inspired his passion to "rectify the world's wrongs." He tried to rid America of the inhumane horrible system of slavery. He knew that it was wrong and believed he could make a difference. Within two years after finishing college started *The Liberal Christian*, a biweekly publication to begin the process.

In 1845, May became the pastor of the Unitarian Church of the Messiah in Syracuse, New York,. He fought for the equality of free Black people in his own congregations. Pastor May demonstrated his commitment by allowing the slaves to sit in the front, as opposed to the segregated rear pews area.

He also fought the Fugitive Slave Law of 1850 by making announcements during his sermons. Not only did he voice his opposition, but he also shared information on fugitive slaves in the area and took up collections on their behalf.

May served in the struggle against slavery by providing aid to escaped slaves along the Underground Railroad route. He was a part of a network of safe houses, safe havens, and resting spots for weary slave travelers heading North. He had many enemies for his strong stance against slavery, support for his beliefs that schools should be racially integrated and coeducational, and fighting for racial equality. May assisted Prudence Crandall in the 1830s when she wanted to open a boarding school for Black girls. The overwhelming majority of the town's people opposed. The opposition was led by a local white supremacist, Andrew Judson. Residents of Canterbury, Connecticut, through the state legislature, made it illegal for Prudence to run her Canterbury Female Boarding School, Young Ladies and Little Misses of Color.

In addition to fighting for the abolition of slavery, May led the rescue of Jerry McHenry, a man arrested under the Fugitive Slave Law. This incident and other similar actions he participated in preventing the sinful display of racism in our country, led abolitionism's opponents to violently attack May and burn him in effigy.

By the time of the American Civil War, May had long been torn between his commitment to pacifism and his growing belief that slavery could not be destroyed without violence. He felt that the use of force against the Southern rebellion was necessary. He continued his work for racial, gender, economic, and educational equality until the end of his life, on July 1, 1871.

10. **George Fox** was a Quaker. He was born on July 1624 and died on January 13, 1691.

Fox was an early advocate for the abolition of slavery. He is said to have questioned the morality of this inhumane system. In 1657, he wrote a letter to slave-owning Quakers condemning slavery again, this time with a Biblically prepared basis. Fox became widely known and respected as minister. One of his sermons preached in Barbados led to a famous book published in London. In it, he advocated freeing slaves after a period of six years. His analogy was similar to the practices of the "Jubilee Year" observations discussed in the books of Exodus and Jeremiah. However, the acknowledgment of the Jubilee Year was not practiced diligently among the prophets or the people at that time.

Fox also advocated for the humane treatment of slaves and preached and proclaimed that Christ died for all people–Whites, Blacks, and Indians. He insisted upon the necessity of treating the marriages of Blacks like those of Whites. I tried to find out through my research tools and sources what those were just out of curiosity. I was not successful and encourage you to continue to do so if you are interested. In his book, "Gospel Family Order," Fox shared a short discourse concerning the ordering of families, both of whites, blacks, and Indians. Fox's Gospel Family-Order shows little moral indignation about the treatment of slaves in the West Indies.

However, Fox's anti-slavery legacy is said to be ambiguous. He never addressed the "morality" of slavery.

According to Dr. Opal Lee, "Racism at any level in a nation's existence is threatening, but when it embeds its powers in high places of governance and laws, it is most destructive. It defies human intervention. We are fighting against a powerful immoral and dangerous sin."

PART 3

Vignettes of White American Heroes and
Sheroes of the Struggle

After Slavery:
Reconstruction, Jim Crow, and Civil Rights Era

Part 3 continues with more vignettes about Black and White Americans' heroic attempts to unite and erase provisions for racial abuse and disharmony conducted post slavery. The Reconstruction era, Jim Crow laws, and Civil Rights Movement battles were fought by these fearless and courageous Americans too. They tried to move America toward freedom and equal rights, as promised in the Constitution and other legal documents, to all.

THE CHOSEN VESSELS

I believe our ancestors and founding fathers would have been proud of these Americans. During the Civil Rights Era, these White American heroes, sheroes, and organizations united and fought alongside our Black ancestors. In unity, together, they struggled to help our nation live up to the promises of equality, justice, and the human rights of all American citizens.

In an effort to grapple with our history, I would like to share a brief introduction of the names, the lives, and legacies of these great Americans. Not every human being could have fulfilled the calling of these special Black and White Americans. I thank our Supreme Being for them and other unsung citizens.

These vignettes are about American citizens who chose to work together in spite of skin color and racial differences. They lived such rich lives that proved to be so significantly empowering, that they are still relevant today. We want to pique your interest to prompt further research, discovery, and discussion of our rich past. We think of them as Chosen Vessels. All are our American heroes and sheroes. They were on a mission to serve God, our nation, and humanity.

1. Pastor James Reeb was born on January 1, 1927. He died in March 1965. He was a White American Civil Rights Activist.

James Reeb was born in Wichita, Kansas and grew up as a young man in Casper, Wyoming. He was raised in a Presbyterian family but stepped away from its teachings as an adult. He was drawn to the Unitarian church and became a minister in that faith. James Reeb was married to Mary Deason, and they had four children.

Pastor Reeb graduated from the University of Wyoming with a degree in Philosophy and Social Sciences. He later earned a degree in Theology from Princeton Theological Seminary. He was a Unitarian Universalist minister who tried to show support for Martin Luther King, Jr.'s plea to involve the clergy in America's war on human rights.

King knew the need for unity and a strong show of support from his White Brothers and Sisters, in the faith, could empower America's Civil Rights Movement. It was a nonviolent Christian and faith-based protest and movement for equality and voting rights. Pastor Reeb heard King's cry for assistance. He tried to help. As a young White faith-based minister, his presence and prayers were important. He was a strong advocate for social justice and equal rights and was able to accomplish many goals in the movement. Pastor Reeb tried to help his fellow Black Americans in securing the right to vote and seeking to escape other horrible Southern Jim Crow laws. He risked his life and marched along with other Civil Rights Leaders in the South. Unfortunately, in spite of the good he tried to do as a minister and American, while walking back from dinner (with two other ministers) one evening, he was attacked by a group of white supremacists and brutally beaten. Two days later, he died from those injuries.

His murder in Selma, Alabama, by white segregationists, led to even larger protests, from Black and White citizens, all over the United States. His death impacted the nation from the East Coast to the West Coast of America. It moved President Lyndon Johnson to take the dramatic step of addressing Congress and the nation regarding the urgency of the Civil Rights issues and concerns for all Americans. Pastor Reeb's death helped to galvanize support from other Americans to pass the Voters' Rights Act of 1965.

Three men were charged with Reeb's murder. They were acquitted of any charges by an all-white jury on the Alabama state level.

However, at a federal level, they were convicted of violating Pastor Reeb's civil rights.

James Reeb's legacy will live on in our memory as another great American hero who tried to help our country to fulfill the promises of unity and equal rights for all of her citizens. He was nationally known as a martyr when he died on March 11, 1965, in Selma, Alabama. His life helped America to become a more united country as our past Black and White ancestors wanted and expected it to be.

Our ancestry, Black and White, can be proud of his great legacy. I believe he is a true American hero. Share your thoughts:

____

____

____

____

____

2. Viola Fauver Liuzzo was born in Pennsylvania, California in April 1925. She died on March 25, 1965. She was a White American Shero and Civil Rights Activist.   Her mother was a schoolteacher and her father, Herber, was a coal miner. Viola had one sister, Rose Mary. She was not from a wealthy family.

In March 1965, Liuzzo heeded the call for help from Reverend Martin Luther King, Jr. to his White brothers and sisters in the struggle for civil and human rights. King knew that with Blacks and Whites together, this nonviolent battle would have more power and strength in unity. Whites were not readily seen on the battle front of the struggle to enforce civil rights for American Blacks. Yet, King knew that many supported and believed in this nation's vision of freedom for all.

Viola Liuzzo was a young American female who believed in America's vision and wanted to help. Liuzzo left Detroit, Michigan and headed South to Birmingham, Alabama to begin her journey. Here she, intentionally and intensively, began her legacy in the human rights efforts. Consequently, being a White female attempting to work in the midst of mostly Black people, she was scrutinized and checked out by the FBI and other American organizations who were suspect of her motives and good intentions… (Remember the lyrics from "Being Carefully Taught to Hate?") Liuzzo wanted to help America win the war that was being waged to extend civil rights to all people.

She was a dedicated and committed worker in the 1960s. Liuzzo participated in the Bloody Sunday's attempt to march on the Edmund Pettus Bridge. She participated in other Selma marches and helped with coordination and logistics of the movement. While performing the task to transport activists to the airport, she was shot and killed by a white supremacist group. In 1965, at the age of thirty-nine, this young life was snuffed out by fatal shots fired from a pursuing car of Ku Klux Klan members.

Although the State of Alabama was unable to secure a conviction of murder for the four men who were known and charged, they were charged in federal court under the 1871 Ku Klux Klan Act. In September of that year, they were found guilty by an all-white and all male jury and were sentenced to 10 years in prison.

Viola's legacy will live on in the memories of many Americans as a fearless White shero, activist, and martyr. Her name is inscribed on the Civil Rights Memorial in Montgomery, Alabama. Even though she was criticized, ostracized, and hated by many, she was a bright light of hope and inspiration for Dr. King and others in the struggle. Viola tried to help America become a truly great freedom-loving country. Her death helped spur passage of the 1965 Voting Rights Act. Her life helped America to become more united.

Our ancestry, Black and White, can be proud of her great legacy. I believe Viola Liuzzo is a true American shero. Share your thoughts:

____

____

____

____

____

3. Danny Lyons was born in New York in 1942. Lyons was a student photographer at the University of Chicago in the 1960s. He is the son of a Russian Jewish mother, Rebecca, and a German-Jewish father, Dr. Ernst Fred Lyons. He grew up in a wealthy family in Kew Gardens, Queens. He attended the schools there.

Lyons is said to have admired the courage of the students who were participating in the Freedom Rides of the South. He hitchhiked to Cairo, Illinois, to become a part of the demonstrations against racial inequality in America. After observing the different actions and experiences, he decided to become a volunteer of the Student Nonviolent Coordinating Committee (SNCC) organization. His skills that he brought to the table were in photography. He spent the next two years at SNCC. This organization became the major channel of student participation in the Civil Rights Movement against segregation and racial discrimination. He photographed student-led sit-ins at segregated lunch counters, boycotts, and other civil rights events across the South. Lyons was SNCC's first Chief Photographer. At significant risk, in many instances, he took practically all of the events this civil rights group held during that time period. His work played a key role in shaping SNCC's image and support in America.

Once Lyons decided to march with the demonstrators to a nearby segregated swimming pool. The demonstrators knelt down to pray as the crowd heckled them. A truck came through the crowd in an attempt to break them up. A young Black girl was hit by the truck. Lyon's captured it. He knew then the value of his part of the movement for then and in the future. His skills were needed.

While in Jackson, Mississippi, and the Mississippi Delta, getting pictures of voter registration workers, he encountered a run-in with law enforcement. He was threatened to be killed and told "we don't mix races down here." Remember the lyrics, "You Must Be Carefully Taught?" …Lyons is said to have claimed a Black grandfather' at that point. On another occasion, his photography played a significant role in securing justice for the thirty young Black girls who were jailed in the Leesburg Stockade scandal. In Americus, Georgia in July 1963, these young girls, ages twelve to fifteen, dressed in their Sunday best, were arrested for trying to purchase tickets to a segregated movie theater in their small hometown. They were arrested and held for 45 days in a cell with one toilet, no beds, no showers…Photos were finally released in leading Black- and White-owned newspapers (*The New York Times, Chicago Defender*, and *Jet Magazine*) of this heinous and despicable crime. It raised the ire of concerned Americans all across the United States of America. Lyons' photos and newsletters helped to lead to their release. He worked in unity with other Americans, Black and White, together, to build a more humane society. Our ancestors wanted this, as well. This part of history needed to be recorded to share with future generations. Danny Lyons' legacy will live on in the memories of many as a talented young energetic great American hero. Our Black and White ancestors would be proud of his contributions to our American society's growth in social justices. As we approach our Semiquincentennial celebrations, we can see progress in America's struggle to move forward.

The Leesburg Stockade was a dark and evil real-life event that occurred during the Civil Rights Movement in the 1960s. It could easily be a setting for a horror movie. Very few Americans then or today even know about this horrible real-life experience committed in America on American soil. There is very little research available, but it was said that: In Georgia, a group of African American teenage and pre-teen girls were arrested in a small rural town in Georgia. They had gone to the small, but segregated movie theater, to purchase (not rob or overthrow) tickets to see a movie. More than a dozen girls, some as young as 12, were taken to the county jail before being transferred to an old, abandoned stockade in Leesburg, which was approximately 30 miles away from home. The girls were held there without beds, a working shower or toilet. The girls' parents and loved ones had no knowledge of their whereabouts for weeks. They were imprisoned without charges for 45 days in poor conditions in the Lee County Public Works building, in Leesburg, Georgia.

Danny Lyons' brave and courageous work in harmony and unity, is an example of Americans working together to possibly save the lives of these girls. The parents of these girls received an invoice for the days they were held in captivity. According to the stories we heard, no one was ever charged for the "kidnapping" of these girls. It is another true "American tale of racism that ran 'unchecked and inconsequential.' By the way, some of these women are still alive leading up to the Semiquincentennial in 2026.

To learn more about this event, you can visit the following sources:

- Stolen Girls: The untold story of the Leesburg Stockade Girls

- The Leesburg Stockade Girls – StoryCorps

- Leesburg Stockade - Wikiwand

- The Stolen Girls (1963) - Blackpast

Our ancestry, Black and White, can be proud of his great legacy. I believe Danny Lyons is a true American hero. Share your thoughts:

____

____

____

____

____

4. Claiborne Paul Ellis was born on January 8, 1927. He died on November 3, 2005. He was born and raised in Durham, North Carolina. He was a white American segregationist turned Civil Rights Activist and trade union organizer.

Claiborne Ellis worked for several years at a gas station before he got married and had four children. The financial strain he experienced in trying to take care of himself and his family led him to "blame Black people." These thoughts might have been influenced by his father's association and loyalty to the Ku Klux Klan. While working at the gas station, he met others who were of the same mindset and invited him to become a part of the local KKK group. He became a very active member, and due to effective organizational and leadership skills, he quickly rose in the ranks to Exalted Cyclops. and local leader of a Ku Klux Klan group in Durham, North Carolina.

As he grew older, Ellis began to feel disillusioned with the notion of the American dream. In 1971, the Durham City Schools faced considerable turmoil because of court-ordered desegregation. The state AFL–CIO received $78,000 in grant money from the Department of HEW to address the school system's racial policies. A community organizer, Bill Riddick, motivated by fears of violence among the students, organized a series of community meetings. They were called a charrette… where the entire community, all races, came together to try to solve this problem. The first step was to create a steering committee, representative of their community. Ellis served as co-chair of this diverse, predominantly Black and White, (a few other races were represented), committee on school integration. He soon became so involved in working in harmony with this interracial group, he resigned from his position as Exalted Grand Cyclops of the KKK. After resigning, Ellis went back to school and earned a high school diploma. He then became a union organizer and played a key role in organizing workers in Durham's construction industry. By 1980, Ellis was the manager of the International Union of Operating Engineers in Durham, which was predominantly Black.

Leaving the Klan and abandoning their mission was easy to do, once Ellis was placed in the position of working with people who he thought he hated! The focus was in direct contrast to what hate groups in America intended to have its citizens believe. To become an advocate for civil rights meant that Ellis was criticized and ostracized by his friends and family members. But the results of his work are to be praised highly. He was carefully taught against hate! He lived his well-received lessons!

His legacy will live on as a White American who contributed to the Civil Rights Movement in his own way. He was a segregationist turned Civil Rights Activist and trade union organizer working together in unity for America. Our Black and White American founding fathers and ancestors would be proud. Ellis demonstrated what changes in divisive attitudes of working, together, as a team can do to move forward.

Our ancestry, Black and White, can be proud of his great legacy. I believe Claiborne Ellis is a true American hero. Share your thoughts:

____

____

____

____

____

5. Juliette Hampton Morgan was born on February 14, 1914. She died on July 16, 1952. Juliette was the only child of Frank and Lila Morgan; the family was very wealthy and prominent in Montgomery, Alabama.

Juliette attended the University of Alabama and became a librarian and Civil Rights Activist in the deeply segregated Southern state of Alabama. Even though she was raised in a segregated environment, early on, she pushed for integration of schools and public places. As a writer, Juliette frequently spoke out, adamantly, against segregation and the acts of injustice that she witnessed against African Americans. She was fearless in her determination to speak out against racism and used the "power of the pen" to call attention to racist bullying tactics used by certain hate groups. Juliette wrote incendiary letters to editorial sections of popular newspapers and her stance was not popular or appreciated.

Juliette often wrote for the Montgomery Advertiser, a local newspaper, supporting federal anti-lynching laws and the abolishment of the poll tax. Jim Crow practices and the lack of equality practiced against Black citizens were targeted topics which she exposed. She continued to point out the harsh and cruel realities of post-slavery struggles of Black people.

Juliette joined Black or White organizations that promoted social justice, equal and civil rights, and other reform to help African Americans. Sometimes she would be the only White member in the group! She joined an interracial prayer group, The Fellowship of The Concerned, and the meetings for the group had to be held in African American churches. The White churches said it was a violation of the city's code to hold integrated meetings in their facilities. She was also a member of the Southern Conference for Education Fund and the Southern Conference for Human welfare.

Juliette was chastised, ostracized, and castigated by her white community for her anti-racial views, lifestyles, and these patriotic expressions. The racial hatred and venomous actions hurtled against her became so overwhelming and burdensome. She was targeted by segregationists who broke out windows in her home and maligned her property, including the burning of a cross in her front yard. Unable to bear the strain caused by the unrelenting retaliation from people who did not love the American idea and its promises of equality for all, she gave up. The unceasing pressures caused by her views, from her own race, contributed to her taking her own life, but Juliette made a difference in her lifetime.

Her legacy will live on in the memories of those who knew how much she loved America. However, she wanted our country to live up to her promises to all of her people. She happened to see and witnessed the inequities being netted out to Black citizens and chose not to ignore or join in this atrocious and unfair behavior. She wanted and tried to make a difference. She was not afraid to challenge racist bigoted behaviors, even in her own hometown. Juliette fought acts of injustice she witnessed among the voiceless people who were

Americans, too. Even though all did not appreciate her then, now there is the Julliette Hampton Memorial Public Library in Montgomery, Alabama. It stands in her honor as a Civil Rights Activist who gave her life to help fight for a stronger America.

Our ancestry, Black and White, can be proud of her great legacy. I believe Juliette Hampton Morgan is a true American shero. Share your thoughts:

____

____

____

____

____

6. Michael Schwerner was born on November 6, 1939, in The Bronx, New York. He was a White American Civil Rights Hero and Activist. He died in Mississippi in 1964. Michael Schwerner was raised in Pelham, New York, in a family of Jewish heritage. He was the second of two sons of a father who operated a wig manufacturing plant and a mother who taught high school biology. Schwerner attended Pelham Memorial High School. Afterwards, he went to Michigan State to become a veterinarian. He later transferred to Cornell and majored in Sociology.

Michael Schwerner led a local Congress of Racial Equality (CORE) group on the Lower East Side of Manhattan, called "Downtown CORE." He also participated in a 1963 effort to desegregate Gwynn Oak Amusement Park in Maryland.

As activism increased in the South of America, many young patriotic people from all walks of life wanted to get involved. Michael was one of those youth who wanted to make a difference for America's efforts toward equal and civil rights for all.   He had majored in Sociology at the University and knew he could help.

Michael volunteered to work for National CORE in Mississippi. Bob Moses, a Harvard educator, and leader in the Civil Rights Movement, welcomed him. He assigned Michael to organize the community center and activities in Meridian.

Schwerner and his wife tried to establish contact and unity with White working-class citizens of Meridian and went door-to-door to speak with them. He also organized a Black boycott of a popular variety store until it hired its first African American, under the principle of "don't shop where you can't work." Schwerner's arrival in Mississippi as a (CORE) field worker, aroused the curiosity of white supremacists. After he organized this successful boycott of this store in the city and voting registration efforts for African Americans, there was more animosity than curiosity. (Remember, you are not to help…You Must Be Taught to Hate) Schwerner became extremely innovative and active in working for voting and civil rights for African Americans in Mississippi. He worked to make the American dream a reality for some who had been disenfranchised, in spite of promises of equal rights.

While helping African Americans to get registered, and the other work needed to promote civil rights, he was killed in response to his efforts. He was one of three CORE workers killed in rural Neshoba County, Mississippi, by members of the Ku Klux Klan. Schwerner's two co-workers were killed, also. These deaths of James Chaney, Andrew Goodman and Michael Schwerner sparked national outrage and helped spur passage of the 1964 Civil Rights Act.

They later became the subject of the movie "Mississippi Burning." Michael Schwerner's legacy continues long after he and his co-workers Andrew Goodman and James Chaney were murdered on June 21, 1964.

Our ancestry, Black and White, can be proud of his great legacy. I believe Michael Schwerner is a true American hero. Share your thoughts:

____

____

____

____

7. Andrew Goodman was born on November 23, 1943, in New York City. He died in Neshoba County, Mississippi in 1964. His family, as well as the community in which he was raised, was devoted to intellectual and socially progressive activism.

Andrew Goodman was the middle offspring of three sons. The other two siblings were Jonathan and David. He received his early education from the progressive Walden School. Goodman's interest in learning more about racial and economic discrimination started early. At Walden's, he was responsible for bringing Jackie Robinson, the great talented Black athlete as a speaker at his school. As a senior interested in equality and civil rights, he and a friend interviewed several citizens to find out more about the causes of poverty. They interviewed coal miners, union representatives, and state congressmen. With this information, he and his classmate were able to reason that to protect the poor, structural changes within the capitalist system would be necessary. He continued his appetite for helping the downtrodden and voiceless African Americans who were disenfranchised. He wanted to make a difference in registering voters, an American civil right, for elections in Mississippi.

He was one of three Congress of Racial Equality (CORE) workers murdered in Philadelphia, Mississippi by members of the Ku Klux Klan in 1964.

His legacy continues long after he and his co-workers Michael Schwerner and James Chaney were murdered by a white supremacist group, KKK, on June 21, 1964. The deaths of these young talented men sparked national outrage toward this group. It helped spur passage of the 1964 Civil Rights Act. They later became the subject of the movie "Mississippi Burning."

Andrew Goodman's legacy lives on through the contributions he made to the Civil Rights Movement. His parents started the Andrew Goodman Foundation. Its mission is to promote the values Andrew had lived and died for: universal civil rights, social justice, free speech, and social and political activism. The foundation is led and promoted worldwide by his brother David. His legacy and ties to helping America in extending civil rights to all her citizens, lives on through his Andrew Goodman Foundation. What is the legacy of those who were guilty of murdering these three young Americans who wanted to move our country forward?

Our ancestry, Black and White, can be proud of his great legacy. I believe Andrew Goodman is a true American hero. Share your thoughts:

____

____

____

____

8. Joseph T Reiff graduated from Millsaps College. He later received a doctorate degree from Emory's Candler School of Theology. Dr. Reiff's impact on the Civil Rights Movement was nonviolent and impacted many citizens inside and outside of the Methodist church.

On January 12, 1963, Pastor Rieff, and a small group of White Methodist pastors in Mississippi composed a bold statement entitled "Born of Conviction." The document could have led the way for other reserved or reluctant White Methodists to engage in America's ongoing conversation on the need for racial equity and justice amongst all of her peoples. The document was intended to remind church members of the Methodist Discipline's claim… that the teachings of Jesus "permitted no discrimination due to race, color, or creed." Also, as ministers and leaders of the Gospel, they made it clear that they were in opposition to closing schools rather than to integrate. These were major challenges to the arch-segregationists' point of view during this time of social unrest and upheaval in America. Race, even in the church, has always been an issue in America.

The ministers knew the usual or past accusation for these types of statements. There would likely be accusations "of being communist" or communist supporters. It was language used as a tool against Civil Rights Activists, Black and White. So, each of the pastors signed and documented their opposition to Communism to accompany their presentation of efforts.

It was not well-received by the highly segregated population and white supremacists, during this time and place in the South. There was intense resistance to change, even amongst church congregations. Only a small amount of secretive support was shown to the signers of this document that was intended to offer support and guidance to its congregants. Needless to say, even though they were clergy, leaders, men chosen by God, there was a "swift backlash." There were many reports of violent threats against them, dismissals and evacuations of their pulpits, cross burnings in parsonage yards, and other such "non-church" racist actions and reactions to their message. It was in the local and national news daily. As strong as these pastors were in their conviction and beliefs, within a two-year period of time, only eight of the original twenty-eight withstood the challenges they faced. The rest moved on.

Later on, still trying to help in the struggle, Pastor Rieff wrote a book, "Born of Conviction: White Methodists and Mississippi's Closed Society," centered around his unforgettable lived experiences. The book tells the story of "the twenty-eight" White clergy's attempt to make a difference in race relations in America. In it, he outlines the high cost a group of Methodist ministers paid for their involvement during the Civil Rights Movement era.

Pastor Reiff's legacy will live on as a gigantic effort toward changing racist attitudes and beliefs in the church and amongst determined church people of the South. As a result of taking this risk, they lost their jobs as ministers and leaders. Many lost neighbors, parishioners, friends, and families who were in opposition to receiving instructions of Christ's teachings. They, of course, faced many of the same fears and threats as other American freedom fighters in the struggle to make these United States of America a country for all its people.

Our ancestry, Black and White, can be proud of his great legacy. I believe Pastor Joseph T Reiff is a true American hero. Share your thoughts:

____

____

____

____

____

9. Reverend Bruce Klunder was born on July 12, 1937. He died on April 7, 1964. Bruce moved with his family to Oregon where he was educated. He earned his bachelor's degree from Oregon State University in 1958 in science. Bruce W. Klunder met his future wife, Joanne Lehman, while attending the school. They married on December 22, 1956 and had two children. In 1961, he earned a Bachelor of Divinity from Yale Divinity School.

After college, Klunder and his wife moved to Cleveland where he was hired as assistant executive secretary of the Student Christian Union at Western Reserve University. He quickly became involved in civil rights. He was passionate and committed to helping to make a difference. He felt he had a special calling for this work. He headed the local chapter of the Congress of Racial Equality (CORE) organization.

Klunder frequently marched and demonstrated for fair housing and against other racially segregated public facilities. Whenever there was a protest against injustices in housing and education, Klunder was there. He was among the (CORE) members who demonstrated at the state legislature for a fair housing bill. He also demonstrated against unfair and unjust racial discrimination in hiring and employment practices for CORE.

On April 7, 1964, Klunder and his fellow demonstrators were opposing the construction of a segregated school in Cleveland, Ohio. He was run over by a bulldozer and killed while protesting the building of the school; the operator was not aware of his presence.

After his death, Klunder's family continued their activism. Joanne and the children participated in civil rights demonstrations, school board picketing, and Vietnam War protests. The schools that Klunder and his fellow demonstrators were opposing on April 7, 1964, were still—eventually—built. The Southern Poverty Law Center celebrates his life of activism, sacrifice, and teaching that his widow has carried on in the six decades since.

Our ancestry, Black and White, can be proud of his great legacy. I believe Reverend Bruce W. Klunder is a true American hero. Share your thoughts:

____

____

____

____

____

10. James Peck was born on December 19, 1914, in Manhattan, New York to a wealthy clothing wholesaler. He died on July 12, 1993, in Minneapolis, Minnesota. James Peck was a White American Civil Rights Activist who was born into a wealthy family and practiced nonviolent resistance during World War II and in the Civil Rights Movement.

While in college, Peck became known as an individual thinker. He was considered to be a social outsider and preferred the company of scholarly intellectuals. To prove a point to show support for his anti-racist beliefs, he committed personal acts of defiance toward his mother and his classmates to aggravate their racist attitudes.

He participated in at least two peaceful demonstrations supporting the Black cause. The Journey of Reconciliation in 1947 and the first CORE Freedom Rides in the early 1960s. Many sacrifices were made as a result. Peck was seriously injured when a group of Klansmen jumped on the bus of freedom riders and brutally beat the entire group. Peck was so savagely beaten, that he was immediately taken to a hospital for help. It was segregated and he was turned away. He was later served at a different hospital, Jefferson Hillman. His battered facial injuries required over fifty stitches.

These Freedom rider campaigns helped open the doors for many Black people who had been denied eating privileges in restaurants and other eating places that White American citizens enjoyed.

James Peck was the leading activist in the "Proxies Campaign" where he protested at business stockholders' meetings. He was influential in getting these big businesses to integrate and hire workers of color. He was called a Civil Rights Hero by many, during his lifetime. Other great Black Civil Rights Leaders, Bayard Ruffin, A Philip Randolph, and others were only a few that sought his wisdom, skills, and support.

James Peck advocated for nonviolence civility in the struggle for equal justice in America. Just as many Black demonstrators and protesters experienced, he was arrested and jailed over fifty times for his efforts.

Our ancestry, Black and White, can be proud of his great legacy. I believe James Peck is a true American hero. Share your thoughts:

---

11. William Moore was born on April 28, 1927, in Binghamton, New York. He died on April 23, 1963, in Kenner, Alabama.

William Moore was a White Civil Rights Activist and a postal employee. He earned a name for himself and enormous respect in both roles. He attended Johns Hopkins University. While in graduate school, he suffered a mental breakdown and was diagnosed with schizophrenia. Later, he became an advocate for the mentally ill and for the civil rights of African Americans.

Moore joined the Congress on Racial Equality (CORE) in the early 1960s as a volunteer in the struggle for civil rights. His intentions were to march to each capital to hand-deliver his letters. Moore engaged in three civil rights protests of major notoriety. He always marched individually, or alone.

On his first march, he walked to Annapolis, Maryland, the state capitol. On his second march he walked to the White House. He arrived there at about the same time that Rev. Martin Luther King Jr. was being released from the Birmingham jail after protests in that city. His letter to President John F. Kennedy said that he intended to walk to Mississippi and "If I may deliver any letters from you to those on my line of travel, I would be most happy to do so."

For his third protest, he planned to walk from Chattanooga, Tennessee to Jackson, Mississippi

and deliver a letter to Governor Ross Barnett urging him to accept integration. He was wearing sandwich board signs stating: "Equal rights for all & Mississippi or Bust." About seventy miles into his march, Moore was interviewed by a reporter, Charles Hicks. The radio station had received a tip on Moore's location outside of Gadsden, Alabama. Concerned about Moore's safety on this rural stretch of the Highway, Hicks offered to drive him to a motel. Moore insisted on continuing his march, alone.

Less than an hour later, a passing motorist found Moore's body just down the road. He had been shot twice in the head at close range with a .22 caliber rifle. The gun's ownership was traced to Floyd Simpson (a white man), whom Moore had argued with earlier that day. No charges were ever filed against him. Moore died a week short of his 36th birthday.

 His letter was found and opened. In it, Moore reasoned that "the White man cannot be truly free himself until all men have their rights." He asked Governor Barnett to: "Be gracious and give more than is immediately demanded of you...." After his death, friends attempted to deliver Bill Moore's original letter to the capitol in Jackson, Mississippi. Bob Zellner, a longtime activist and first White Field Secretary of the Student Non-Violent Coordinating Committee, was with them in that effort to meet Governor Haley Barbour. Barbour declined to meet with the party.

 On the 47th anniversary of Moore's murder, April 23, 2010, a memorial plaque in tribute to him was unveiled. It is permanently on display at the Greater Binghamton Transportation Center, across from Kennedy Park and down the street from the Martin Luther King

Jr. Promenade, in New York. A pioneer in civil rights, Moore is the only White person featured in Investigation Discovery's Injustice Files in 2011.

Our ancestry, Black and White, can be proud of his great legacy. I believe William Moore is a true American hero. Share your thoughts:

____

____

____

____

____

12. Jonathan M. Daniels was born on March 20, 1939. He was murdered at the hands of other Whites on August 20, 1965.

Daniels was a seminarian student and a Civil Rights Activist. Born in the North, he was educated at the Episcopal Theological School in Massachusetts. He was a good student and graduated as valedictorian of his high school class, and later graduated from the Virginia Military Institute.

After facing and overcoming many obstacles in life, Daniels felt he had received a calling from God. Daniels was one of the helpful ministers who had responded to Rev. Martin Luther King's request from the White clergy to help in the struggle. This brave and courageous young man headed South to Selma, Alabama. He knew there was risk involved, but he wanted to assist in the nonviolent protests for voting and Civil Rights Movement. At significant risk, Daniels took groups of African Americans to the local Episcopal church in Selma. He was met with some degree of approval. He continued to try to integrate the citizens by working in other roles.

Late one evening in 1965, Daniels waited for transportation from the jail, from which he had been in for six days. He, a White Catholic priest, and two others decided to purchase sodas. They were confronted by hate-filled Whites; a part-time law enforcement officer and part-time construction worker killed young Daniels. He was trying to shield another co-worker, (who happened to be Black) from Tom Coleman's gunfire. Unfortunately, the assault was deadly. Mr. Coleman attempted to assassinate the priest as well. He was seriously wounded as he ran from the gunfire.

Jonathan Daniels, and this incident, was viewed all over America. The young seminarian's death generated an abundant overflow of media attention and support for the Civil Rights Movement. Even in death, his life made a difference.

Jonathan Daniels' legacy will show a committed young Godly life dedicated to civil and human rights. One of five elementary schools in his hometown is named after him. He is recognized annually as a martyr, in the church's Day of Remembrance calendar.

As we approach the 250th birthday of our relatively new nation's Semiquincentennial, let's prepare to celebrate and commemorate the lives of these heroes and sheroes who fought vigilantly to bring America to this place at this time.

Our ancestry, Black and White, can be proud of his great legacy. I believe William Moore is a true American hero. Share your thoughts:

____

____

____

____

____

PART 4

Summary and Conclusion:
Pressing Forward in the Fight Against Hatred, Violence, and Divisiveness

Part 4 offers a summary and a conclusive statement to encourage American citizens to continue to press forward in the fight against hatred, violence, and divisiveness. All parts of this project are designed to encourage, uplift, and prompt further civil discussions, continuous positive dialogue, and oral and written research by our talented precious young scholars and their friends.

I, as a Black American octogenarian, believe, as most would, America is a wonderful place to call my home. My beginning is probably the most unique of all the races who inhabit this land. From the unforgettable human and financial sacrifices of my ancestors to present day opportunities and experiences, I know that this is my home. I am grateful to my Supreme Being for this blessing. I believe America is far from a failed project or finished work. I believe America is a great country with its diverse multicultural, multigenerational, multireligious groups, and ever-expanding population.

Her wealth and resources are abundant, yet it is not seen by many as Utopia. Remember, the homeless, drug addicted, incarcerated, disabled veterans, poverty ladened, forgotten elderly, foster and adopted children are a few American citizens who make up our diverse population. They are vivid expressions and targeted populations in need of our care. And only hate, misunderstanding and ignorance will lead us to think "they are all a bunch of no-gooders." Some are a reason we remember little about the wars we slept through while they were on the front lines... Many more are mentally ill, and families tried to seek help for them early on but were not able to navigate a complicated system designed to allow only a few in. Many did just give up on life because they believed that they had no reason not to do so. America's attention, given in these areas instead of racial infighting, conflict, and wars, needs to be revisited and re-adjusted before the Semiquincentennials can be celebrated fully. Valuable time and effort with more pressing needs of other sufferings amongst our citizens can and should be made.

Whatever appears to be "Utopia," feels like Utopia, walks, and talks like "Utopia" must be shared in a fair, just, and equitable way amongst its citizenries. It cannot be seen as a nation who shares her many gifts and blessings in one group in the community in abundance and denies another community group these same gifts. Even more repugnant is that the denials are based on race and skin color…reasons these American citizens have no control over or from which to escape. It is racism. Resources and opportunities being issued out to one group in abundance, while another group is being denied in abundance, is un-American. It is a racist practice that denies our nation's people access to equal and equitable opportunities in this freedom loving country. It breeds hate.

A HISTORY LESSON REPEATED: THIS TIME, THE "BROWN" FUTURE AMERICANS

It is said that our nation is built on faith-based values and timeless principles. For over 250 years, it has worked toward managing this diverse group of people. Its major challenges have been to integrate and unite the two dominant races,.one Black and the other White. There is a third impressive, talented, and massive in numbers group, on our borders, literally, as we speak. This group, so far, will be recognized as the Browns. *Can our past help America to prepare for the diverse populus that is knocking at our doors? What can our past teach us to prepare for this group?*

I see this as a special and exciting time to enter into our 250 years celebration! This is even more exciting to welcome diversity within a diverse nation! Their populations are increasing in numbers, almost daily. We in America know what this is like to have experienced the total rejection or acceptance of more diversity in our nation. We are living this experience!!! History has prepared us to be a model "for just such a time as this." It is important that rules from previous governing documents be learned and applied in the processing of all of our citizens and future citizens. America must welcome this new group of potential doctors, teachers, lawyers, scientists, chefs, craftsmen, business owners, 'willing laborers, and so many other honorable and helpful professions and careers.

These "new" Americans cannot be taught to hate. Americans that are already here know that they cannot show hatred and divisive attitudes toward these new "soon to be" citizens. It is important that none of this conflicts or departs from our established faith-based values and principles that are morally uplifting. They must be taught, formally and informally, about America's vision of freedom and equal rights for all of her citizens. They must be assured that equal laws of protection, duties, and responsibilities will be enacted, observed, and respected by all. Our laws apply to all citizens and are mandatory in a peaceful functioning diverse society like the United States of America. America is far from a failed project or finished work. Maybe they can introduce additional ways to work together and demonstrate to us how to get along in spite of racial and skin color issues!

As we approach the Semiquincentennial, the country faces many challenges. However, number one, we believe, has been with us for over a couple of centuries now. It is the challenge and continuous struggle to root out the sin of systemic racism in "high places." I believe there is a distinct difference. Racism amongst decision-makers, authority figures, politicians, religious heads, and other leaders who play major roles in shaping opinions and attitudes are the primary targets. It is an ongoing experiment at a time spoken of by the old prophets, Nehemiah and Isaiah…They prophesied that a time would come when we would not know the difference between "good and bad": That is a scary place to be! When America cannot afford to pacify every group, or every color, she must be capable of implementing and relying on strong laws. I believe they must be built on Biblical principles and values. Once they are understood and accepted through our democratic processes, they must be carried out equally. "Woe unto them that call evil good, and good evil; that put darkness for light, and light for darkness; that put bitter for sweet, and sweet for bitter!" (Isaiah 5:30).

We need laws and they must be respected and accepted by the majority of people. We need laws with consequences applied equally. If that cannot happen due to a divided people, that too is scary. Americans must overcome the evil forces that cause our citizens to feel divided, resentful, and distrustful of each other. We are vulnerable and ripe for invasions and destruction of our democracy, from within and without. "The world is watching" has many messages attached to it.

The world sees our nation as an example. They should, because these united states, acting as one, is a leader and a role model.

It is a diverse institution that thrives on that fact. It is one of our greatest commercials. It is a "melting pot" of what the world has to offer…its diverse cultures, people, and languages. Can our democracy work? Can we blend and unite? Can we integrate our diverse society? Can we live together harmoniously? The world is waiting to see. It is amused by our marches, protests, insurrections, and great racial divisiveness. Our generations to follow must deal with it effectively because the races and populations are increasing. They must be prepared to overcome a lot of the prejudices and discriminatory situations caused by different races and skin color. Unity must be our focus and our goal to help erase and replace the division and distrust amongst our citizens.

We all must become more optimistic in our daily lives. "Self-help, self-confidence, and self-determination can move you to enjoy this present way of life in America. We need to help ourselves and other Americans to rise above the levels of poverty. No law-abiding average American should work on a 40-hour work week job and still be living in poverty, or worse. Someone is being taken advantage of in salaries and wages earned, or "taxes and rents" being charged… or something. Find someone you trust to help you to figure your situation out if you cannot rise above the miserable state of poverty during this era or proximity to the Semiquincentennial. Something that is amiss can very likely be helped with guidance and counseling.

Feelings of not belonging, refusing to let someone else dictate your levels of comfort, defining your own pain and annoyances, should be your decision as a citizen, right? But allow me to encourage you to seek a comfortable space in this nation. I believe you can find one. Believe in America! How? I can only tell you what I know has worked for me. (I encourage others to tell you what has worked for them, if theirs is different…). One thing for certain is…you must find a faith-based anchor and support to help define your purpose in life. I have all of the materialistic comforts and things that I need. I have achieved much in life.

So many blessings including living well past my "three scores and ten" found in Psalm 90: 10. But I want to share with you that my greatest help and gifts come from knowing God. He is, among many other things to me, my friend, a counselor, and a light in dark times in America. He does not teach me to hate.

Reject pessimism and adversities that you cannot change in America, right now. As a citizen of this free country with so many other resources and opportunities, this list should be minimal. It should grow smaller and smaller with age and maturity. Know the difference between "doors that are closed at the moment" from those that will very likely open later, for your good, as well as America's good. Voting and participating in our democratic system can be rewarding. Own your part of America that you feel good about! It does not have to be like anybody else's. It could be *your* home, *your* place of worship or play, y*our* job, *your* career, or employment. Find your love and level of satisfaction with who you are…" the skin you're in!"

- ✓ Prepare yourselves to enjoy as much of America as you can and deserve.

- ✓ Go to school, college or receive training that will keep you well out of poverty.

- ✓ If one opportunity doesn't work out for you, choose another.

- ✓ Keep knocking, a door will open for you.

- ✓ Keep seeking, and you will find most of what you are looking for in America!

We can achieve common ground, improve our country, and pass our freedoms to the next generation by embracing these virtues and principles. Always remember to teach *against* hate.

ABOUT THE AUTHOR

Dr. Elizabeth Grady Branch

Elizabeth Grady Branch was born in Jacksonville, Texas in 1942. She attended Alberta Street Elementary and Frederick Douglass High schools in her hometown. Dr. Branch graduated from the segregated (but dearly loved) Fred Douglass High School in Jacksonville. Her job and career fields were limited in this small struggling town. Standouts included migrant cotton picking, waiting tables in small cafes, field hand, and occasional maid work. However, she found a way to escape the drudgery of poverty through education. She attended Jarvis Christian College in Hawkins, Texas. Her degree was in Elementary Education and English. She later attended Texas Southern University in Houston, Texas where she received a Master's in Developmental Reading. Her Doctorate degree was received in Higher Education from North Texas State University in Denton, Texas. It has since been renamed, the University of North Texas.

Her career after college afforded her a new lifestyle and many blessings and means to escape poverty. The successful accomplishments of becoming a teacher, a college administrator, and small business owner (day care, tutoring center, and an author) gave her immeasurable joy and opportunities! Through her church, career, and community, she has served on many boards and in many areas where she could live a different lifestyle as well as give back to those in need.

Dr. Branch was the first Black woman chosen to lead the Fort Worth's Mayor's Commission on The Status of Women in her city. She was president of the Texas State Association of Black Personnel in Higher Education. She is a past president of the Fannie Mae Heath Cultural club under the historical umbrella of the National Association of Colored Women's Clubs, founded in 1896, the oldest African American secular organization in existence today. She holds lifetime memberships in TABPHE as well as the NAACP.

Dr. Elizabeth Grady Branch has published several books and manuals to help juveniles, young adults, and women to make better choices. Some of these titles include the Man in The Mirror, Working Women in The Winners Circle, Vocabulary Matters, and Reading Skills for Culturally Diverse Students. Choosing to Lift Every Voice and Sing, was released in 2022. It is a book of short seminars to encourage youth to take advantage of the opportunities America has to offer in spite of adversities. Her latest publication is: "A

Workbook of Selected Activities to Accompany Chosen Vessels: Uniting Of the States of America Before the Semiquincentennial."

Elizabeth married her college sweetheart, James "Boogie" Branch, Sr. They have three children, six grandchildren, and two great-grands, Miss "Nova" and Miguel.